Advance Praise

"*What You Lose on the Roundabout* has the charm of *Bridget Jones*, the quirkiness and humor of *Little Miss Sunshine* and the drama of a Robin Cook medical mystery."

Jennifer Donelan, reporter/anchor WJLA-TV, Washington, DC

"Christina Weaver paints a deeply honest, often witty, and sometimes painful look at a life that has been struck by Parkinson's disease. Her story is a rollercoaster of human emotion and contemplation about one's place in life."

Don Rush, News Director, Public Radio Delmarva

"*What You Lose on the Roundabout* is a remarkable accounting of courage, empathy and love. It validates the depth of the human experience in its capacity to convert tragedy into an added value of life. Christina's true story is both enjoyable reading and a testimony to the challenge of modern medicine and those who are destined to serve. It will evoke laughter, anger and tears. You will want to share her story with friends, colleagues and loved ones."

Jeanne Craig Sinkford, D.D.S, Ph.D., author, Dean Emeritus, Howard University, Washington, DC

"A brutally honest memoir, a literary autopsy of the soul – eloquent and touching, at times disturbing – a story of frailty and redemption, of love and forgiveness – of what it is to be human, steeped in the human condition. I loved this book. So will you."

Harold Schmidt, playwright, author, director

"Totally authentic, I can picture it all. I like Ike. You will too. I want to shake his hand and say thank you."

Frank Inglesia, a person with Parkinson's

"A stunning illness memoir that rises well above the plethora of others because Weaver, with her photographer's eye, catches the small moments, the humorous moments, the painfully honest moments that are all too often eclipsed by the illness story itself. Most importantly, she never loses sight of the love story, complicated and controversial as it is, that underwrites every scene."

Maribeth Fischer, prize winning author, writers' advocate

"*What You Lose on the Roundabout* is an inspiring page turner I had a hard time putting down. Healthcare workers will particularly appreciate this family's challenges..."

Marguerite Cyr, RN, MSN, Clinical Specialist,
Washington Hospital Center

"A weaver in more than name only, Christina Weaver creates a rich tapestry of moving experiences and observations invaluable to both mental health workers and laymen."

Evelyn Epstein, MSW, LSCWC, President-elect Washington
Society of Psychoanalytic Psychotherapy

"Christina Weaver shares her very interesting life in an honest and memorable way. After a lifetime of being trusting and trusted, and taking risks, she turned her normalcy upside down, lost the trust of her family, even her own, and then learned a new truth. One for all book clubs."

Joyce Stafford, retired teacher, book club member

"It's my recommendation for a great read, perfect for a get-away weekend, especially at the beach."

Ryan Deck, Lieutenant, Sea Colony Beach Patrol

What You Lose on the Roundabout,
You gain on the swings

Christina G. Weaver

James M. Heller
(content editor)

Copyright © 2007 by Christina G. Weaver

What You Lose on the Roundabout *is a memoir. All the situations described and people are real. Some names and places have been changed to ensure confidentiality. The dialog reflects my best recollection of how conversations transpired. Some timing of events was changed to fit the flow.*

ISBN 0-7414-4125-X

Cover design by *Paprika Creative.*

Back cover photo by Bill Chapman.

Front cover and interior photos from family files.

Published by:

INFIN∞ITY
PUBLISHING.COM

1094 New DeHaven Street, Suite 100
West Conshohocken, PA 19428-2713
Info@buybooksontheweb.com
www.buybooksontheweb.com
Toll-free (877) BUY BOOK
Local Phone (610) 941-9999
Fax (610) 941-9959

Printed in the United States of America

Printed on Recycled Paper

Published January 2008

Author Acknowledgments

I can't thank my family enough for putting up with the changed person I became. Especially my husband, Ike, who promised my Dad he would take care of me, and despite my best efforts to the contrary, succeeded magnificently. Our son, Greg and his wife, Liz and our daughter, Kim, and her husband, Stan appear in the book. Ike and I must have done a lot right because nobody could have a more supportive and loving family than you guys. Ike's daughter and my stepdaughter, Jerdel Hardy is recognized for stepping in just when she was needed and before being asked. We treasure Jerdel, Anarda and Chimere.

My parents, Eileen and Peter Long, made me who I am. They gave me a childhood in which I knew nothing but love and security. They showed me how to reason, laugh often, and stiffen my English upper lip. They allowed me to fly away before they were ready and they grew to love Ike. Pat Wade is my dear cousin in England, whose love, courage and memories, I cherish.

And Dan, we needed each other for a short period in our lives. Good luck, my friend. I look forward to standing in line at your book signing one of these days.

The Players Club is valued for introducing me to the world of music, open mic nights and *lower case blues.*

My friend and fellow writer, Billy Taylor, was enormously helpful in reviewing my original manuscript.

Lastly, I am indebted to Jim Heller, without whose expertise and encouragement the *The Third Wheel* would have remained a manuscript and my experience would remain forever incomplete.

For Ike, my rock

Kim, who broke the spell

Greg, who believed me

Lauren, Zoë, Symone & Nina, our future

&

The young doctor, my hero

1

My Tattoo

"A tattoo, now that would wake me up," I thought.

The coupon I won for a free tattoo sat on the dashboard of my trusty old Saturn for six weeks, out of sight, out of mind. But I'd braked suddenly and it had fallen on the passenger seat next to me.

I was so tired. I just couldn't keep my eyelids from shutting. I could have stopped for a coffee, a Red Bull, a walk on the beach, or even called my husband, Ike, and asked him to come and get me. Those would have been the normal things to do.

But once the idea for a tattoo came to me, it became a mission: the only thing that would prevent me from falling asleep at the wheel as I drove the nine miles back home. I called the phone number on the coupon.

It was mid afternoon and already a bummer of a day. Just a little while earlier, I drove up the coast road from Bethany Beach to Rehoboth in Delaware to drop off an artist friend. He had been helping me and the owner of a small exotic plant shop, with an open house. My two folding card tables covered by a single white plastic table cloth were set up in the front of the shop. I was surrounded by the aroma of orchids and the different textures, sizes and shapes of bonsai trees. On, under, and all around the table were hundreds of my photos that I hoped to sell. My artist friend was in the back room. I paid him for his time and supplies so he could entertain the crowds of children who, like the rest of the world, never materialized.

The no-shows even included my own kids, Greg and Kim, and their families. Starting their week of vacation, they made it clear I should be building sandcastles with my granddaughters, not helping a down-on-his-luck shop keeper and an eccentric, starving artist. It was a day that I tried really hard to make succeed and the let down deflated my stamina.

* * *

"Ancient Art Tattoo," answered the voice. "Yes, we're open and Peggi's available."

Peggi is a living reflection of her discipline and the holder of the "1986 National's Best Tattooed Female" award. She practices in a small arcade off the main highway. Her studio reminded me of a beauty parlor, bright and clean, with seats to wait and magazines with titles like *Prick* to look at. There were large catalogs filled with pictures of potential tattoo designs on a long, chest-high shelf. A slight whiff of incense along with a soft harmony of wind instruments infuses the atmosphere.

"Christina, welcome, you can look over here while I get ready," Peggi suggested as I wandered in. "See if you can find something you like."

At fifty-seven, I was feeling a bit out of place. I rarely wear makeup or jewelry, my ears aren't pierced, and I've never even owned a pair of jeans. Hardly the tattoo stereotype! But I was as resolute as a smoker buying a pack of cigarettes.

I looked through a catalog of flowers, hearts, yin-yangs and snakes and glanced up at the wall behind the counter. A poster-sized Peggi displaying her body festooned with elaborate and colorful designs grabbed my attention. There were tattoos everywhere, from her toes to her neck line. I wanted to walk up closer to examine the detail but somehow that seemed inappropriate.

I peeked in the first booth and watched a bald, muscular tattooist, with multiple rings adorning each ear, intently needle the shoulder of a slender male customer whose lanky pony tail had been swept to the side.

"He'll be with me forever," the man said as his late father's face took shape on his exposed scapular.

"Come on back," said Peggi. She wore an easy smile and pixie haircut that confidently matched her unique body artistry.

I handed her the coupon I won at our local Grammies, where poets, singers and musicians compete. "You were great. I love your poetry and was so happy that you and Factor were winners."

Her nephew played electric guitar in the heavy metal band that I shared the loud applause with at the end of the evening. I wondered if he'd used his winning coupon for an extension of the dragon's fiery breath reaching under the rolled up sleeve of his tee shirt.

"So what will it be?" she asked. "I could do a permanent eye liner if you like. That way you'd never have to bother penciling your eye lids again. It's becoming very popular."

"In fact," she added, "it would accentuate your eyes behind those hip glasses of yours."

I beamed. I loved my new glasses. I had been short-sighted since I was a child but I'd never had a pair like these before. They were a psychedelic flat purple and gold color with tinted, graduated lenses and as light as a feather. I'll never again have those ugly little marks on the side of my nose, I thought, when I first tried them on.

"I'm a word person, Peggi. I want my tattoo to make a statement so when people ask me, I can teach them about something important. Can you do, 'Think Clone, Think Cure' for stem cell research?"

"Sure, where do you want it?"

"Somewhere visible. How about on my right wrist so it won't be covered up by my watch? And would it be possible to do two little stick figures, one in a wheel chair and one walking with arms raised in celebration of being able to move again?"

"No problem," she said. "By the way, how is your Parkinson's?"

"Okay, the medications are keeping it in check. But I saw the video of me performing at the Grammies. I just hate how I can't stop my mouth grimacing. That's one of the side effects of the meds you know. That, and suddenly sending me into a sleepy stupor when I drive."

I sat as still as I could in Peggi's chair for about an hour as she worked her craft. I watched her painstakingly create the design on a transfer and place the paper lightly on my skin. I nodded as she looked at me to confirm the location was just right.

I saw the ink stain from every needle prick gradually take form. I heard her soft slow breaths and saw her tongue escape the corner of her mouth as she concentrated, bending low over my wrist. I noted how the design of her own tattoos changed with every flex of her hand, extension of her arm.

I felt the contrasting temperatures of tiny trickles of capillary blood with the tingle of the alcohol wipes she used to pat the site clean. I observed the narrow line of reddened swelling around the circumference of each imprint.

Most of all, I marveled that I felt no pain.

The pony tail guy got ready to leave. "Thanks, man," he said. "This is perfect for Father's Day."

Damn. Tomorrow was Father's Day, the whole family would be around and I had forgotten about it. I'd let Ike down again. More than thirty-five years married, a wonderful son and daughter, and I'd been much too busy to think about mundane subjects like Father's Day. People needed my help, after all.

"Could you add something for me?" I asked Peggi as she finished the final "e" in cure. "Is there room to put my husband and my initials below? 'C & I', showing we are in it together."

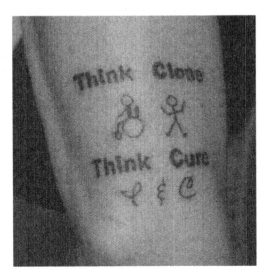

She did everything, just the way I asked.

"Take care," she said, as I walked out.

* * *

"Take care." How I hated that expression. One of the last things my Dad had said to Ike before he died was, "Take care of Christina when I'm gone."

Nobody talked about taking care of me before I got Parkinson's. I always prided myself on being self-reliant. I loved my Dad and my stiff-upper-lip English heritage. I loved Ike and his warm, open-minded African American ancestry. They were each so different yet bonded by a love of me. I hated that they both thought I needed to be taken care of.

* * *

I didn't go straight home. I drove to the trailer where the members of the band, *lower case blues*, live. They were all under twenty-one when I met them at a street festival the year before. Their frenetic yet soulful blues energized me and I felt useful as I helped them build their website. I went out to see them play as often as I could.

"Look Jake," I said. "See my tattoo."

His short, black, spiked hair was tousled from being in bed all day after a late night gig. "It's cool," he commented. "Does Ike know?"

Of course Ike didn't know, I thought as I drove home, sun roof open and *lower case blues'* demo CD swirling funk around my mind. After all, I didn't know myself until the idea popped into my brain.

I was actually surprised, and frankly a little irritated, that nobody at home thought my tattoo was cool. They didn't seem to know what to say.

"It isn't real, is it?" asked Greg, hopefully.

"Of course it's real, indelibly etched in my skin for ever."

Kim pointed her finger towards my wrist. But she couldn't quite make herself touch it.

"It's an early Father's Day gift," I volunteered by way of explanation. "It's for stem cell research, it's an important statement. Surely you understand?"

"Right," sighed Ike.

By now it was almost eight o'clock. The dinner dishes were already washed up and leftovers were in the fridge. My kids, their spouses and their lovely little daughters left to go to their lodging nearby. Their dismay with my tattoo's contribution to the day was poorly camouflaged by artificial smiles. Even more, I detected a weird combination of anger, embarrassment and pity. I didn't mind them being angry or embarrassed but the pity got to me.

Only my granddaughters kissed me goodnight.

"I might as well go to bed too," I told Ike who was sitting on his corner of the couch where he watched TV every evening.

"Right," he sighed again.

But all was not right.

And the night was far from over.

2

Diagnosed

Michael J. Fox called his memoir about having Parkinson's disease, *Lucky Man*. The title annoyed me when I first heard it. He must have had a pretty miserable life, I said to Ike, if he thinks having Parkinson's is being lucky.

* * *

Midway in my nursing career, I attended a conference where the attendees, mostly nurses and social workers, listed life-changing events and discussed them with a partner. The idea was for us to realize that common place things to us, like a new diagnosis, hospitalization and surgery could be momentous to those we cared for. The more such events you have to deal with at a time, the higher the score would be on a stress scale. Sounds simple, but when patients and families complain about what seem like trivial things, it helps you think what else may be going on.

I listed marrying Ike in 1967, the arrival of kids (Greg was actually born on the first Earth Day in 1970), deaths of loved ones, and being raped. Also, societal events like the riots of the sixties, Viet Nam where two friends died, and the advent of AIDS. And tragedies that you'll never forget where you were when you first heard the news, like the deaths of John and Robert Kennedy, Martin Luther King, Christa McAuliffe, and John Lennon.

There is before and after completing nursing school, getting a masters degree and a series of promotions, and eventually the transition from nursing management to a management consultant with a platinum frequent flyer card. All of these have impacted me. All fit together like patches in a quilt. Some are bright, some dark, as many as possible are touched with humor, and all are imperfectly placed together with a variety of blanket, daisy and cross stitches. I've always done my best, found something to laugh about, and moved on.

But the real "befores and afters" for me have been coming to America from England at age sixteen. And then, those fateful words when I was forty seven, "I think you have Parkinson's disease."

Before America, I grew up, an only child, in Cheltenham, a rural town in the heart of the Cotswolds. Click that mouse in your mind and watch the monitor: grassy hills dotted with sheep, golden fields of wheat enclosed by short limestone walls, cottages with thatched roofs, and every house with a flower garden in the front (roses in the case of our house) and veggies in the back.

Imagine an all-girls school with pupils wearing gray skirts, red v-neck sweaters and striped ties. Consider that everyone you know is middle class of Anglo-Saxon, or occasionally Celtic, heritage and from a two-parent household. I knew only love, laughter and openness from my parents and didn't know there was any other way. That was my environment, and my fortune.

After school every day, I rode my bicycle home, drank a cup of tea with my Mum and did several hours of homework. On Saturday mornings, I volunteered in an old peoples' home and at eleven o'clock went to a teenage coffee dance at the town hall. In the afternoon I spent a couple of hours in the library picking out my reading selection for the next week – autobiographies of socially minded heroes, like

Florence Nightingale and Albert Schweitzer, were my favorites.

On Sunday mornings I looked forward to walking in the local countryside with my Dad. Our favorite place to walk was on top of Cleeve Hill. From different vantage points you can see all of Cheltenham, with its easy to recognize church spires, school cricket grounds, and the large industrial brick building where Flowers best beer was brewed. To the northwest is the Vale of Evesham with its rich soil and prolific orchards, asparagus and strawberry fields, and on a clear day, in the distant horizon, are the gray hills of Wales. We lived forty miles from Wales yet I've never been to the country where my Mum was evacuated during World War II. She was a working class London girl, in love with my Dad since she was thirteen and he was twelve. She hadn't liked Wales then, nor ever wanted to return! I think the real reason she disliked it so much was that the elderly couple in whose rural house she was billeted, refused to allow her to smoke.

Both my parents smoked when I was young. In fact a well-repeated tale from my childhood relates my Mum's smoking to me. From all accounts I was a miserable baby who cried a lot. One day, at her wit's end, she called the doctor. As was the practice in those days, the young doctor came to the house. I yelled my lungs out for him too, proving the validity of my mother's complaint. The doctor and my mother walked out into the garden. He lit up a cigarette and gave one to her. "You've got a difficult child here," he confirmed, perplexed as to what to advise. "Just have a smoke when she cries. It will calm your nerves."

Smoking may have helped her get through my babyhood but not enough to ever convince her to want more children!

Eight years later, the first surgeon general's report came out with its warning of the dangers of cigarettes. My Dad read the information aloud from the Observer newspaper. "Eileen," he ended, "we must give up smoking. The facts speak for themselves."

He literally never smoked again, although he was never without candy in his jacket pocket. And I, of course, never smoked for I was my father's daughter. He was the most intelligent person I have ever known, a logical man who found religion illogical and whose humor was self-deprecating. I relished our discussions about politics, God, and whatever else was on my mind.

Mum never gave up smoking. After all, a doctor had given her permission! It took a third stroke to wipe out her memory of the habit, after she already needed to be cared for in a nursing home. Fortunately she died before Dad was diagnosed with emphysema, no doubt from years of close encounters with second hand smoke.

One Sunday, Dad made an announcement. We had finished eating our normal English roast beef and horseradish sauce lunch with Bisto gravy over roast potatoes, Yorkshire pudding and freshly shucked peas. Mum was serving Dad's favorite "pud" (short for pudding and rhymes with should), lemon meringue pie, when Dad dropped his bombshell.

"I've been assigned a three year tour in Washington. We'll be leaving next month."

I was excited to be going to America, sad to be leaving my friends, and nervous about the unknown. It wasn't until I was standing on the upper deck of the Queen Mary, sailing past the Statue of Liberty, watching grown people standing in silence with tears running down their cheeks that I suspected the enormity of the change I was about to experience. The feeling was confirmed by the coincidence of the first music I heard blaring from a loudspeaker on the docks of New York as we awaited our baggage: Aker Bilk's *Stranger on the Shore*.

* * *

Before Parkinson's I was comfortable and self-assured. Ike and I owned nothing when we married but we worked hard, went back to school, plotted our career paths and shared child-raising responsibilities.

We were both healthy, rarely took days off from work and had a wide circle of good friends. Everyone knew me as a planner and organizer. I had a reputation for gathering facts, examining options, making decisions, always having a back up plan, and never regretting what might have been. My Dad once told me he was so lucky because he had a career he loved. "Me too," I told him.

Ten years after being diagnosed with Parkinson's I still struggle with question that starts so many new conversations, "What do you do?" To me, it remains as basic a question as "Who are you?"

* * *

It was 1993 when I started to trip over things and walk ever so slowly. I had been working for a healthcare technology and management consulting firm based in Long Beach, California for seven years. Before that I was the vice president of nursing at a medium sized hospital in Virginia and before that I had worked for seventeen years at the Washington Hospital Center in DC. That was where I had gone to nursing school.

At the time, I had two clients, one in Cleveland where I led quality improvement teams in five hospitals and one in

San Francisco where we selected a new information system for their surgical suite. That was typical, a different day, a different city, a different project.

Most of my colleagues were guys and I found, after decades in nursing, that I enjoyed working with them. It was a woman vice president, however, who told me shortly after I was hired what was required to be a successful road warrior. "You need balls to do this kind of work. You've got to dazzle clients with brilliance when you know what you're talking about and baffle them with bullshit when you don't. The trick is understanding that you know more than they do and believing that you have the capability and resources to get the job done better than the competition."

On her desk, next to a box of business cards was a wooden sign with the etched words, *"Illegitimati Non Carborundum."* I couldn't work it out. "Don't let the bastards get you down," she told me with a smile.

"What happened to you?" asked the OR Director when I turned up around noon on a Monday after an early morning cross country flight from Dulles. The extra large Band-Aids on both my knees, bulging under my hose, and the scrapes on the under sides of both wrists were conspicuous beneath the skirt and sleeves of my smart business suit.

"Just a stupid fall while I walked the dog," I replied.

I didn't tell her it was my third stupid fall in a month and that I was a bit concerned. Many of our meetings were in a conference room lined with mahogany bookshelves holding years of bound *Archives in Surgery*. I often worked in there alone, reviewing vendor responses to our detailed Request for Proposals. Guessing correctly, I found the latest *Merck Manual*, the medical reference book, at the end of one of the shelves and stuck it in my brief case for hotel room reading that evening.

There is a *Merck Manual* for the layman, called the Home Edition, but all self-respecting nurses use the original medical version. I had a feeling the problem must be neurological. Multiple sclerosis was a possibility but then I decided I was too old for that to be likely. Maybe a brain tumor? A little knowledge, as they say, is a dangerous thing!

It didn't occur to me to go to my family doctor. Instead I made an appointment with one of the best neurology practices in the D.C. area. Kim worked with this group while she was in nursing school and she suggested the doctor she liked the best.

"We'll need to do tests to rule out anything else, but I think you have Parkinson's. Your right arm doesn't swing when you walk. That's a telling sign." I heard little else that he said.

Parkinson's hadn't crossed my mind. I was too young. When I was a head nurse on a busy medical floor we'd had lots of Parkinson's patients. Not only were they all old, but they all looked the same. I couldn't remember one individual face; just stooped backs, stiff limbs, shaky hands, drooling mouths and, worst of all, expressionless faces. *"Shells of Themselves,"* I called them later in a poem. Oh my God.

It's a good job I knew the way home and the traffic was light because tears streamed down my face all the way. "Ike, you won't believe it," I blurted on the car phone. "I have Parkinson's. That's why I've been falling. Have you noticed my arm not swinging? When will you be home?"

He came home immediately, just as he had thirty years before when I'd been raped. He has always been there when I needed him.

Kim was still living at home. Even though I traveled virtually every week of her high school years, we were really close. Sometimes I think that in our nightly phone chats, she opened up to me more than if I were a stay-at-home mum. I love the fact that she had chosen to follow in my nursing footsteps. She came directly home from class that day to learn the results of my appointment. "Oh, Mum," she said when she saw my red face and swollen eyes.

We hugged when I told her that I was doomed. She was still in the pre-clinical stage of nursing and didn't know enough to remind me of the disease's slow progression. My life would be far from over.

I went through the testing phase including a brain scan, skull x-rays and various blood and urine tests. Ike came with me to hear the results and to just be there. As we sat, arms intertwined, in the waiting room, I noticed a news bulletin about a Parkinson's meeting on an adjacent table. I studiously ignored it. I was already sure that Parkinson's was my fate; I saw my symptoms in my second read of the *Merck*, yet still hoped for a tiny, completely operable benign tumor. How stupid of me.

"The tests are all negative," the doctor said. "So that rules out many other diagnoses. Unfortunately there is no specific test for Parkinson's. We have to confirm it's nothing else and go by symptoms. The next thing is to try some initial medication and see if you start to do better. Improvement would indicate you have Parkinson's. If not, we'll look for something else."

"What exactly is Parkinson's disease?" Ike asked.

"It is an illness that usually affects people after the age of sixty, more men than women. Christina is young but it can affect people in their twenties and thirties. There are three cardinal symptoms: rigid limbs, resting tremors and slowness of movement. It is a progressively disabling condition for which there is treatment but, at this time, no cure."

"What causes it?" Ike continued.

"The problem is caused by an area, deep in the brain, called the basal ganglia not producing enough dopamine. Dopamine is a chemical, known as a neurotransmitter, which helps send messages from the nerves to the muscles to smooth movement and coordinate actions."

"But why does Christina have it?" Ike persisted. "Is it inherited?" This was my biggest concern. I didn't care how I got it; I just wanted to hear that I couldn't pass it to my kids.

"We really don't know why one person gets Parkinson's and another doesn't," he said gently. "In some populations there does seem to be a genetic thread but generally not. There is a lot of research going on."

"Doctor," I started. "You know my daughter, Kim, recommended that I see you. Well, she tells me that one of your colleagues is a Parkinson's specialist. Would it be prudent to get a second opinion from her?"

He agreed and I met my new doctor a week later. After examining me, she asked me if I had a tendency to be constipated ("yes"), if I had ever smoked ("no"), if my sense of smell had become less acute ("yes") and if my legs were restless, especially later in the day ("definitely").

"In fact," I said, "flying home from seeing out of town clients has become embarrassing because I just can't keep my legs still. It's quite disruptive for anyone sitting next to me."

It turns out this combination of attributes is pretty common in people diagnosed with Parkinson's. The diagnosis was confirmed.

My luck, so to speak, was to have acted early on my symptoms. They started me on a medication called Eldepryl to help protect the production of dopamine. It worked for a while. I started to move faster again. I could walk with my head higher without fear of tripping.

* * *

My diagnosis coincided with the middle of my Mum's five-year purgatory in the nursing home. I visited her twice a year but waited until the third trip after getting the news before breaking it to Dad. I would have preferred him not to know but I didn't want him to accidentally hear from anyone else. He caught sight of my one day's vial of about twenty pills before I'd thought of the right intro.

"The worst, the absolute worst." He sat back in his chair, his long legs stretched out in front, and put his tankard of beer on the table next to his ever-filled bowl of peanuts. He removed his glasses, wiped his eyes with his handkerchief and closed them. I went into the kitchen to check on lunch and pour myself a gin and tonic. Dad was focused on his weekly cryptic crossword puzzle when I returned.

The day before I was to fly back, he asked me for more details. Then he said, "It's a wicked disease. Last Christmas I got a card from my old golfing pal's wife. He was always ready for a quick nine holes. Not any more. They had to move closer to their son because she can't manage him by herself."

* * *

I sought out some literature to help me deal with my new reality. One of the books that affected me greatly was *Saving Milly* by Morton Kondracke. Mr. Kondracke's name was familiar from *The McLaughlin Group*, a political jousting tournament that I watched regularly on Sunday TV. "Nonsense," I often uttered as he bantered with his sparring partners.

"Did you know Mort's wife has Parkinson's?" Greg asked. It turned out his best friend worked for the Capitol Hill newspaper, *Roll Call* where Mr. Kondracke was executive editor.

"Really? I think that I saw his name as next speaker at the Parkinson's Association meeting. The topic has to do with the politics of Parkinson's. I'll go."

By the time *Saving Milly* was published in 2001, I was unable to read much more than a page at a time, very slowly with finger stroking the lines. I leapfrogged through much of the content, thankful that someone as knowledgeable about government as Morton Kondracke, is such a passionate gadfly. I leapfrogged until I reached the last chapter, *Losing Milly*.

All of my concerns about the future, losing my intelligence, being unable to communicate, wanting to die sooner not later, and wanting Ike to have a life and not be a caretaker were Milly's current reality. A reality expressed with such honesty, dignity and love. I've read every word in that chapter more than once, one page, then a break to get my eyes refocused, then the next.

I went to Milly Kondracke's funeral. There, I shook Michael J. Fox's hand. I wished I had half of their bravery. And I was thankful to have Ike as my Mort.

* * *

Unlike many "Parkies," I was extremely fortunate to be employed by a firm that was both understanding and also had excellent disability insurance. I've learned other people who are diagnosed with chronic illnesses are afraid to tell their employer for fear of repercussions.

After a couple of continuing fast-paced years, it became harder to keep up with the physical demands of the job. My doctor prescribed some new medicines and recommended I stop traveling as much. "Stress exacerbates symptoms," she wrote on a prescription sheet. Not traveling in a consulting world can be the kiss of death so I decided to be proactive. Recognizing a need, I created a job description for a regional director of human resources and presented it to my boss.

It became the best role of my career. I was responsible for hiring and staffing the many talented young associates our growing firm needed. From me they learned the practical side of consulting and how to make the most of each assignment. Always I encouraged them to draw on their experience to write for professional journals.

"Do like I do, take your report and turn it into an article," I used to say. "It's good for you and good for the firm."

In return, my computer knowledge and skills grew just by trying to keep up with them. Their work-hard, play-hard attitude energized me, but what really made me love the job was the reality of making a difference in many of their professional and personal lives. Whether guiding one through promotion or helping another think through concerns about adopting a baby, I was involved and appreciated.

There was a downside. Moving sideways in a consulting firm virtually eliminated the possibility for promotion to vice president. I had a lot of support from the vice presidents I worked with, and sympathy when every six months the list of promotions, absent my name, was announced. At the time I felt let down and had to stay on my guard to keep my disappointment to myself. In the long run, however, it was probably just as well as becoming a vice president involved the serious commitment of personal money to company stock. The firm was going public at the time, increasing the risks of stock ownership. Given the short period of time I had left in the firm, the right decision had been made.

* * *

By the time I was ready to retire, my regime of medications had become more complex. I took Sinemet CR 25/100 four times a day. Sinemet is more akin to dopamine than any other drug available. It has extended quality of life for millions of Parkies. But eventually Sinemet becomes less efficient; there are frightening differences in "on-off" periods, and the side effects become as difficult as the symptoms of the disease.

An off period can strike quickly. You can be moving or thinking normally one minute, and the next you're just stuck. I hadn't experienced a complete mobility "on-off" yet but I had seen Parkies literally stalled as they walked across the room. They knew they wanted to keep walking but they didn't get the message from the brain telling them how.

Some of the other side effects were known collectively by the medical term, "tardive dyskinesia." This means that there are involuntary, obvious, sometimes painful, movements of one's arms, legs, face and mouth. I found myself grimacing, tightening my mouth, and sucking in my lips. The meds also cause the mouth to get dry so between the two problems I frequently suffered with a line of mouth ulcers on my lower lip against my teeth. The dryness also leads to cavities. After we moved to Bethany my new dentist found thirteen that needed to be filled. I found keeping my mouth open very difficult so she used a special rubber device so I couldn't accidentally bite down.

As an adjunct to the Sinemet, I was also taking Mirapex 0.5 mg four times a day and Tasmar 50 mg three times a day. Their function is to boost the potency of the Sinemet and make its effect last longer. My neurologist warned me about Tasmar after I had been taking it for about a year. "Studies have revealed the drug has the deadly but rare side effect of producing acute, fatal liver failure," she said in her matter-of-fact way.

"The government now requires me to provide my patients who take Tasmar a consent form to sign, acknowledging you understand the risks, freeing me of responsibility if you do get liver failure, and agreeing to have your blood tested for liver functioning every two months. I have to sign the form also and it gets sent to the Center for Disease Control in Atlanta."

"What would you do?" I asked. She shrugged indicating the decision was mine to make. Her responsibility was to provide me the information to make the decision for myself.

"Tasmar's working well for me," I said. "The odds against liver failure seem pretty good. I'll sign the form."

Yet despite this regime of state-of-the-art drugs, I kept struggling to keep up with work. It took me longer to get through the massive amount of information. I couldn't focus and draw conclusions. The pile in my inbox grew to a small mountain. Multi-tasking became impossible.

I worked fourteen hours each day but did less than I had in my normal ten to twelve. I moved awkwardly and tired quicker. On two occasions, I came home from trips with bruises and scrapes after tripping over. My pride was what hurt the most, especially when colleagues saw what happened and rushed to help me. But worst was my difficulty reading. The words seemed to shake along the lines. There were times I got emotional and even cried at work – so out of character.

Shortly before I retired, I read *Living Well with Parkinson's* by Glenna Wotton Atwood. Her story made me sad. It also gave me strength. It reminded me of me. She was a teacher; her daughter worked in one of the hospitals where I consulted in Maine. She described her life as being normal and happy; the very words I use to describe myself. I lent it to Ike, Greg and Kim to read. I wanted to thank her for writing the book, and to tell her personally what an impact her words had on my outlook of Parkinson's.

The publisher gave me an address. Her daughter, or maybe it was a niece, took the time to write to me and let me know the family appreciated my comments, but alas Ms. Atwood had recently died of pneumonia. She lives on through her words.

The ninth chapter of her book starts with an old Sanskrit verse. I used the same verse when I wrote my *"Final Page from Christina"* in the firm's newsletter.

> *Look to this day!*
> *For yesterday is already a*
> *Dream*
> *And tomorrow only a Vision*
> *But today, well-lived,*
> *Makes every yesterday a Dream of*
> *Happiness,*
> *And every tomorrow a vision of*
> *Hope*

May we all have the wisdom to live each day, as well as possible…

Along with retirement came honors. I was given the firm's first Lifetime Achievement Award. It was in the form of a framed record album, the Eagles' *Hotel California*.

"Relax," I was told on stage. "You can check out any time you like, but you can never leave!"

My colleagues in the DC office gave me a wonderfully generous roast and a piece of glass sculpture I later called "my wave of change". I woke up the next morning to find trickles of tears running down the sides of my face and pooling in my ears. Reflecting on the previous evening of fun and laughter at my expense, brought to mind an Irish wake; lots of food, drink and people remembering the good times. But at a wake the person being celebrated knows nothing. At my retirement roast I mourned my own premature loss of society's symbol of worth: work.

During the six months surrounding my retirement, my list of "life-changing events" included: Dad's death, Greg and Kim each getting married, the exchange of my British passport for a vow of allegiance, and our relocation from Northern Virginia to Bethany Beach.

The first time I heard the word "bereft" spoken aloud was when my mother died. "I am bereft," Dad agonized, his arms embracing the hollow in his chest as he walked round and round their small living room.

Bereft was not too strong a word for the way I felt. Christina, get a grip, I told myself.

3

A Research Subject finds a Kindred Soul

"You have a handsome groupie," the book shop assistant whispered with amusement as she turned away.

I pretended to be busy by starting to write a few lines of a poem when I heard his voice.

"You are doing just what I want to be doing in a few years. May I look at your book?"

"Please do. So you write?"

"Oh yes." He pulled the bulging book bag off his shoulder and lowered it onto the floor next to the wall. "It's all in there, my life in spiral notebooks."

* * *

Bethany Beach, known as the "Quiet Resort", is where we always enjoyed happy family vacations and three-day weekends. Ike is my senior by nine years and he had been happy to retire from the ardor of inner-city psychiatric social work at Saint Elizabeth's Hospital shortly before me. It wasn't hard for us to make the decision to move away from the suburbs to somewhere fresh, different, and yet familiar.

Our home was in a community where most of the houses were wealthy peoples' "summer places". Ike and I were amongst the few "year-'rounders" and we soon made friends with others who, like us, were retired. Life was like living on a never-ending vacation.

I looked so well and happy it was hard for all my new friends, many well above the normal retirement age, to realize the extent of my illness and its effect on my morale. I met most of these lady friends at an indoor swimming pool where we did aquatic exercises three times a week.

Can you imagine how it felt to be the slowest one as we paraded around the circumference of the pool, waving our arms and side-stepping our feet? I was more than a decade under the average age of the group. One lady in particular, Marilyn, became a close friend. She looked out for me like a surrogate mother, saying she felt "swell" when I called to check on her. She said that in my presence she felt younger than her seventy-eight years. Sometimes I felt very old in hers.

They had no idea just how much Ike helped me, how he did all the practical chores around the house, and how he reminded me of the need to eat and sleep. They didn't understand why I still yearned to work, not play, and why the word "relax" had yet to join my lexicon. "Poor me", I would think, "old before my time." It wasn't something I moaned about. I'm good at masking my feelings with a smile and a well-learned stiff upper lip.

Ike gave me my best retirement gift: a three-wheeled bicycle. Bicycles get you from here to there, but whenever you stop to look around or catch your breath you have to put your foot down on the ground. On a tricycle, you can keep your feet on the pedals, stay sitting on the seat totally balanced, look around, chat, and even eat, all without getting off.

It is flat in Bethany, and on good days I could ride as far as the ocean. More than distance, it gave me freedom. I felt the breeze ruffle my hair as I rode to the swimming pool early in the morning. I heard the giggles from my back basket as I gave my granddaughters' rides. I often rode my bike when taking the dog out to do her business. Riding was easier than walking as I didn't have to worry about tripping. I laughed when I heard young children turn to their parents saying, "That lady's got a cool bike!"

It helped balance my body, mind and spirit.

When you retire to the beach, reading the weekly free newspapers becomes a habit. It's how you find out what's going on and realize how quickly you recognize the photos of people you have met. One day a small announcement caught my eye.

"They have Parkinson's meetings about an hour from here," I mentioned to Ike. "Would you be interested in coming with me?"

"Sure."

The meeting was in the community room of a large church. There were about twenty attendees, a leader and a speaker. Several people were in wheelchairs and others had walkers. The carers, as their significant others were called, seemed much more involved than the Parkies, themselves. I hated the meeting. It started late. Ike and I sat on the periphery of the circle. We smiled but nobody offered their name or seemed interested in adding new ones to their telephone lists. I was younger, healthier, and still newly sprung from the corporate world. I didn't want to belong. But who did?

The leader did his best to hold the meeting to its agenda but there was virtually no participation from the group. His low voice made him hard to hear and his visible shakes made him hard to watch.

Yet the journey was worthwhile. There was a visiting speaker from a Parkinson's Research Center at a university medical center, north of Bethany. She told us of a new lifetime study for Parkinson's patients. The study would end with the donation of the participants' brains for autopsy after they died. This research was important because an autopsy is the only way to examine the depth of the brain tissue where the Parkinson's occurs. Perhaps, my being in this study would help doctors find a cure, I hoped.

The speaker explained the study would involve a full day of assessment followed by checkups every six months until the day we died. "You will be asked to complete a form giving us the names of your next of kin who we can contact," she told us.

I realized this was serious business a few weeks later. Kim called. She has the kind of voice that tells you exactly how she feels. "Mum, is there something I should know? I got this form in the mail. I have to sign that I swear I will do my very best to get your brain there within two hours of your death."

"Oh, Kimba, I'm sorry. I haven't even been for my first assessment yet, I never thought they would be this efficient. Don't worry. I intend to be a participant in this study for a long time!"

* * *

About three months after learning of the study, I found myself sitting in one of the hundreds of little, windowless, patient examining rooms in the Movement Disorder Annex. It was seven thirty in the morning. A nurse with a clipboard told Ike not to return until five and that my day would be full of testing to determine my level of my physiological, intellectual and psychological functioning. The information would become their baseline against which to measure my decline for the rest of my life.

Each hour I met with a different physician or technician. I demonstrated my gait, touched my nose with my finger a hundred times, and put pegs in holes to show physical agility. The intellectual tests reminded me of some of the games we'd played at my parents' parties when I was a child. For example, I looked at a tray of items and then had to record the ones I remembered.

Then the examiner told me stories, more and more complex, asking me to repeat them back. I did well with the test in gambling. It was the logic and odds of predicting which card would be drawn next. The tester told me I had done better on it than the staffers had. I don't gamble, but my sense of logic is deeply entrenched.

Psychological testing came last. It included the completion of several multiple-choice questionnaires and an interview with a resident in neuro-psychiatry. I had been surprised by the prick of tears as I answered probing questions about Parkinson's and life in general. In addition to all my life changing events, I had also managed to compress three lumbar vertebrae in a ridiculous accident when I stepped on a little luggage rack to hang a picture in our new home. Not surprisingly, the tacks holding the canvas straps gave way and I dropped about eighteen inches to the hard wood floor. A child would have known I was too heavy for it but I was impatient to see how the picture would look. "You've really done it this time," I said to myself as I heard Ike rush up the stairs after hearing the crash. The injury which left both legs tingling and numb from my hips to my toes required two surgeries to fix and a lifetime of being careful ahead.

"Do you ever think about wanting to die?" the resident asked. As always, I responded openly.

"Yes, I've thought about suicide," I answered. "Not for the immediate future, of course, but definitely as an option for when my well being becomes another's well keeping. Wouldn't you feel the same?"

At the end of the day, I waited to meet Dr. Leo, the study's primary investigator, in his office. The room was cramped and packed with stacks of books, journals, patient charts and family photos. The walls were decorated with framed certificates and awards. I was impressed. I sat on a low comfortable chair on the other side of a high desk adorned with a desk top computer, printer and scanner.

I was quite pleased with how the day had gone. I had enjoyed the different challenges of the tests. Best though, was the interaction with the individual team members. I wanted them to know that at least at this stage of the Parkinson's game, I still could exchange ideas as a colleague more than as a patient. Oh how I missed the hospital environment.

Dr. Leo was a tall gangly man, with wavy, salt and pepper hair and wire rimmed glasses. He walked in fast, carrying the results of my day's testing. He popped a peppermint lifesaver in his mouth, and offered me the tube. I took one and he jumped into conversation without taking the time for pleasantries.

"Mrs. Weaver, your Parkinson's medical regime seems to be working very well for you. It is important that you keep up with your exercises in the pool and, of course, take your medicines regularly. We have one concern. The testing tells us you are really quite depressed. You just do a great job of masking it. We think you would benefit from seeing a psychiatrist who is especially trained to practice with Parkinson's and Alzheimer's patients."

Well, I protested, looking up at him from my lowly seat, with all I've been through recently surely it's quite normal to be a bit depressed? Plus, to be in a study that culminates with the examination of my brain on autopsy, isn't exactly an upper! He smiled, benevolently.

I thought through the idea. It did seem prudent to go along with the suggestion of getting counseling. After all, I wanted to stay on good terms with the research team and they might get offended if I declined their first recommendation. And, depression is known to be a common aspect of Parkinson's. That darned dopamine, I was learning, has a complexity of functions affecting body, mind and mood.

* * *

Since moving to Bethany, it hadn't taken me long to replace spreadsheets with photography, bulleted memos with poems, and team meetings with writing groups.

In an ironic twist of fate, Parkinson's allowed me to discover my right brain. A spark of creativity resulted in a proliferation of miscellaneous poems and local photos. I needed to start and finish something — to have something to show that I could still be productive.

One day while indulging in one of my favorite new pass times, antique shopping, I came across a wonderful old book called *America*. It was written and illustrated by the author of America's national hymn, Reverend S. F. Smith in 1879. It gave me the structure for what to do with some of those poems and photos I had been working on, and the idea to celebrate the part of the country that I now call home. *Delaware, I Sing of Thy Shore* was the start of my changing attitude.

* * *

Meet the Author, Friday, July 12, 2002, 7:00 PM. The sign in the corner window proclaimed my impending visit for the past week. Book signings, I learned, are important events for authors and bookshops. It was the first time I had ever been the subject of an event and, I confess I was starting to enjoy a little small town notoriety.

Anticipation became reality. The book of poems, photos and anecdotes that consumed my winter was ready for sale.

Even the weather had taken note, and at last early-spring temperatures had turned to summer. The start of the season at the beach, parking meters and the influx of thousands of visitors which constitutes the lifeline for a small seaside town, coincided with my first book signing. It was a good omen.

On Wednesday, my book was featured in the local newspaper. The article concluded it was a "must-have for anyone who appreciates the beauty that surrounds us." I agreed that my little book belongs on the end table of every discerning household across the country, but was a little bothered by the objectivity of the reviewer – an employee of the book shop! Such petty intellectual scruples are easy to ignore, however, when you have two thousand self-published books sitting in the closet under the stairs with costs you would dearly like to cover.

Ike helped me get set up in the entrance of the local bookshop, the one everybody passes on the way to the boardwalk, the beach, ice cream and French fries. I'd been too nervous to eat all day, and the heavy aroma of cooking oil blended with the sharp twang of vinegar, tempting my senses.

"Smile," he said as he departed. He looked through the bars of the white iron railing. "You look like you're in the zoo!" He was going home to his every-Friday-fried-fish supper.

"Maybe someone will toss me a French fry," I retorted.

He was gone. My book was "Christina's thing" to him. With Ike, the Friday fish routine is like reading the newspaper and drinking two cups of coffee every morning: his.

I wished we had more things that were ours. After thirty-five years of marriage, two married children and two granddaughters, we were as committed to one another as the day we were married. We had always been determined to prove wrong the nay-sayers who never expected us, an integrated couple, to last.

I was the conductor and Ike played the drums, tambourine, trombone and harmonica in our one-man band of marriage. Ike was rightly proud of the appearance of our home and garden while I focused on keeping our financial house in order. These differences were becoming more pronounced after we both retired and we shared each other's daytime space.

It is the pattern for people to grow more entrenched in their ways of doing things as they get older. That was true for Ike but not me. I was becoming a creative scatter-brain. It was a challenge for everyone who knew me well, especially Ike. Our roles were changing and the future was uncertain. I blamed all my frailties on my Parkinson's. Sometimes I wondered if I used it as an excuse.

* * *

Fifty blue and gold covered paperbacks, with an oval cutout revealing one of Delaware's famous watchtowers, were stacked in neat piles on a card table. The cover was designed by Liz, my daughter-in–law. These books were incomplete, lacking the flourish of a signature. Next to them was a vase overflowing with pink, purple and lavender hydrangeas, a good luck gift.

I was dressed to match the flowers: a lilac, short sleeve, tee-shirt and flowing dark pink and cream skirt. I had to laugh at myself. My first book-signing event and I looked as though I was ready for tea in Monet's garden! Yet despite the shower of color, only a trickle of customers showed any interest in my $19.95 "must have."

In fact, the event was much more awkward than I had imagined. For the first time, people were going out of their way to avoid catching my eye. Easier, I realized, for them to ignore me than have to say, "No, I'm here to buy *The New York Times* ten best sellers and have no interest in having a little look at your not-quite-coffee-table-sized, soft-covered, forty-eight pages of drivel."

That's when my groupie appeared.

He was tall and lean and had sandy brown hair sticking out from his cap, turned backwards. I noticed the logo on the cap, the University of Maryland Terps. It's not the kind of thing I usually recognize, but Maryland granted both Ike and me our Bachelors' degrees. I own a red tee-shirt with two terrapins doing CPR. He could have been one of our kids' friends a few years earlier – smart, a bit brash, easy to befriend.

He seemed pleased to have someone to talk to. When conversation dragged, he looked in my book, read the prologue and then my poems. Most people remark on the photos that accompany each poem. He only saw the words. And his favorite poem was mine, *Kindred Souls*:

> *In our short lives,*
> *If we are lucky*
> *There are one or two people*
> *With whom there is a bond*
> *Deeper than friendship*
> *More vital than blood*
> *People with kindred souls*
>
> *They laugh at the same silly things*
> *Delight together in the wonders around*

Read each other's mind
And share each other's frailties
Relationships too pure to cause resentment
Too strong for change to tear asunder
Almost "a given" to those near and dear

When apart they have in their mind's eye
Special places to go alone to be together
Places where simple pleasures have brought such mutual
joy

That to recall them is to make time stand still
Like the perpetual ebb and flow of the tide
Waves and hearts beating in unison forever

For ever, never alone
As kindred souls live eternal in our hearts and minds

He read it aloud, without hesitation, ending slowly. Another customer stopped to listen on her way into the store. She bought a book!

"Why did you choose the word, souls?" he said. "Why not spirits?"

"That's interesting you noticed. I struggled with that word choice. I guess soul is a deeper word than spirit to me. The words spirit and spiritual are used so freely now that they just seem to be a bit of a cop-out for people who are uncomfortable with calling themselves religious."

He turned back to the book and focused on the intro page where I wrote about having Parkinson's. There I go again, I berated myself. You can't keep any conversation light any more. Someone makes a comment and you go into a dissertation about belief.

"Hey, isn't this difficult for you? Sitting here touting your book – it's like, this book is you, so personal – don't you wish you could just give it away so everyone could enjoy it? It must be so different for you now that you have Parkinson's."

"How did you read my mind? And how do you know how much I miss my old life?"

He shrugged his shoulders and read another poem. Fifty-five minutes of chatter and six signed books later, he had my phone number and would call if he could come to my weekly writers' group meeting the following Wednesday.

I met his Mom briefly. She acknowledged him talking to me as she disappeared inside the bookshop. I was vaguely aware of his father sitting in their car waiting to drive them back to their beach condo. He told me his parents would be leaving at the end of the weekend, leaving him to stay in the condo alone.

"I'm going home to write," he said. "Watching you with your book makes me really want to follow through with my dream. I have something to say."

His mention of staying in his grandmother's condo to separate himself from his parents' protective hold, and having neither a means of transportation nor apparent job escaped significance in my mind. It did strike me he possessed the criteria I told my kids I looked for in their dates: look me in the eye, converse articulately and – essential – have a sense of humor. I may also have noticed that he had a mischievous twinkle in his grin. Oh, and his rendition of Kindred Souls resulted in a purchase! How could he go wrong?

Eventually, our lively discourse about poetry and life had exhausted his parents' patience and he slung the book bag over his shoulder and hustled towards the parking lot. His parents' weariness of waiting was matched by the infusion of energy his presence had provided me.

"I'll try to come on Wednesday," he yelled over his shoulder before disappearing into the bright light of the street.

"Your groupie didn't want to leave," the book-shop lady kidded me.

"Mmmm," I replied.

There was something about him that clicked in my mind. And me in his too, I knew.

* * *

"How did it go?" Ike asked after we got home.

"Good but kinda slow," I answered, putting Monet's flowers on the mantelpiece.

"I expect you wished Pete could have been there. He would be so proud."

Only Ike called Dad Pete. To everyone else he was Peter.

I hesitated before saying, "Oh and a young guy showed up. He might be interested in the writing group."

It was as much as I wanted to say. It was likely he wouldn't call anyway, although I had a feeling he would.

I couldn't even remember his name.

Somehow, I wished Ike hadn't brought Dad into the conversation.

4

Two Writers

The day after my book signing, I went to a luncheon that was the result of another announcement in the newspaper. This one was about the formation of a new group for people with Parkinson's. Actually, I noticed it in previous weeks' editions, but studiously ignored it each time. Then I received two phone calls and a torn out newspaper page from well meaning friends and neighbors. "Oh thanks for letting me know," I lied each time.

"We're going to have our first meeting next week," a cheery voice said when I called. "It's my idea, I just thought we would all be better off by sharing our experiences and being there for each other." I can't argue with that reasoning, I thought, as I recorded the name of the restaurant and the time in my pocket calendar.

The meeting was disturbing. Each of the other three women was friendly and pleasant and our commonality made for easy conversation without pregnant pauses. The one I related to best was a former librarian. Her husband, the only man in the group and the only one of us without Parkinson's, had wheeled her to our table of five.

I found myself sneaking little looks at her. I cringed as the New England clam chowder dribbled down her chin from a misplaced shaky spoon. Her husband waited for the right moment, when he thought the rest of us wouldn't notice, to dab wayward creamy drips with his napkin.

Another woman rubbed her thighs, much as I do when mine get achy. "I need another Sinemet", she said reaching in her over-sized pocket book. "Know what you mean," I replied.

Collectively, I realized that our faces were comparatively expressionless. Bloody hell, I thought, our faces are becoming as lifeless as shells on the beach.

The refrain "shells of themselves" ran through my mind all the way back home. I didn't say hello to Ike, I just climbed the stairs to my computer and started writing. This is the first verse, it just flowed without thought.

> *Shed shells, once filled with life and purpose,*
> *Now hollow, immobile, flat, and eerie.*
> *Seashells are jostled by the whim of waves, pull of the tide.*
> *"Shells of themselves" are pulled from the car, pushed in wheelchairs:*
> *The dopamine-depleted who haunt the dopamine-deficient*
> *At support groups where they are taken*
> *By weary spouses wearing cheery masks,*
> *For better, for worse, weary, forever.*

* * *

I answered the phone.

"Hi, it's Dan. Remember me?"

So that was his name. And yes, he wanted to come to my writing group. I agreed to pick him up outside the bank that was opposite the condos where he was staying.

He was waiting for me, his cap still on backwards and book bag on his shoulder. He reached in through the open window on the passenger side and have me a high five before getting in.

Our group of writers consisted of several regulars, high schoolers to retirees, and a couple of occasional members. For me, the primary value of the group was its very being. I wrote more and better just because of its existence. I also enjoyed the variety of writing: sweet poems to social commentary, old fashioned short children's stories to psychological thrillers. It was the teenagers' work that impressed me the most. Not only were they amazingly creative and technically strong but they had the insight to give spot on critiques to the rest of our writing. It is this country's great loss that one, Chad Clifton, was later killed in Iraq. "He always wanted to experience what he hoped to write about," his mom told me after she published *A Random Soldier,* a book of his words and her commentary.

On Dan's first night there were five of us sitting comfortably in a circle of armchairs at the back of another local book shop. This one has the additional benefit of serving coffee. Just as a good bartender pours the beverage of choice for a regular, so my penchant for a café mocha, large, skim milk, with cream topping, iced, was rewarded without my needing to ask. That evening it was ready by the time I got to the counter. It made me remember my Dad's center of the universe, the Bayshill Inn in Cheltenham, where his "pint of your best" was always perfectly drawn before he reached the bar.

In addition to my shell poem, I had another new one to read. Inspired by Ike's and my recent vacation to Germany, it was titled *Disquiet* and was about World War II.

After listening to my reading, Dan complimented me and added: "I'm Jewish and can really relate to words of warning about charismatic dictators who blind their people into believing wrong is right. But I didn't realize that there was such a strong continuing feeling about the war in

England. I should have known that." I nodded, pleased that he was pleased with my poem.

Dan listened carefully to the rest of the group's comments. "Is it okay if I read something or should I just listen this week?" he asked. Upon being reassured that he could speak up whenever he wanted, he blossomed, sharing that much of his writing was about global issues, war and peace, humanitarianism.

From the depth of his book bag, he pulled out one of several well-worn, pencil-written notebooks and found what he was looking for. "I wrote this about a year ago," he mumbled. "This is the first time I've shared my writing with anyone." He read fast, as though his writing was unworthy of our time:

> *Return with me to the hollow of night, and the*
> *Anguish of exploration for expression.*
> *How can I explain to you?*
> *How do I convey mystique, the yearning*
> *For the eloquence, of an accomplished poet?*

His reading continued for another three verses.

"You've got a lot there. Read it again, real slow," someone said. Dan complied, concentrating. He frowned when the poem didn't flow as well as he expected and took notes in the margins about changes he wanted to make later.

Next he read one that started: *"We can orbit Jupiter but cannot love our neighbor. Will it take a nuclear explosion to see that an eye for an eye doesn't work?"*

"It is still a work in progress," he explained. It turned out to be just one of many poems started and never returned to, or refined.

I glanced at the others in the group. One of the regulars, a free lance journalist, named Billy caught my eye and nodded that he thought my young friend-in-writing had potential. Another participant indicated he had particularly liked the line *"The yearning for the eloquence of an accomplished poet."*

A sliver of a grin briefly appeared whenever there was positive feedback. Like all of us, he wanted approval and respect. But Dan is also of the generation where it is cooler to pretend you don't really care what other people think. I noticed that he looked at me on occasion as though checking my response to his work, just as I had looked for his reaction when I finished my poem.

Then, increasingly he tapped his foot, squirmed in the chair and sniffed as though we were in the middle of hay fever season. Still his seriousness about his writing along with his friendly smile quickly broke the barrier of being the new kid on the block. By the end of the session he was just one of the writers.

After everybody took a turn reading, Billy reminded me of the next planning meeting for the Writers' Cabin. This project was his baby; it was to be a house where emerging writers could spend three months focusing on their art, and receiving the insight of local writers and visiting authors.

"That sounds great," said Dan. Later, as we got in the car, he asked: "May I come to the meeting, too? The Cabin idea – that would be so perfect, a house where the sole purpose is to write, where you're surrounded by beauty to inspire you and other writers to motivate you to write even better. When do you think it might start?"

I couldn't tell him. The planning process was dragging out but there had been talk about a trial program starting in around six weeks. Regardless of the start date, I cautioned

Dan that the selection process would be quite strict. Yet I was excited that his response to the Cabin was just what Billy had hoped it would be.

"Tell me more about yourself," I said realizing that nothing concrete had been revealed in the couple of hours we had been together.

"Well, I'm the oldest. My brother takes after my Dad, very ambitious, black and white, getting a degree in economics. I never could live up to my Dad's expectations."

"So do you come from a practicing Jewish family?"

"Not really. I mean our whole family, relatives and all, gets together to celebrate the holidays but we're definitely not orthodox. I'm a spiritual thinker. To me existence, nature, truth, beauty are all God. You're spiritual too, I can tell."

"No, not me, I'm certainly not religious and I don't think of myself as being spiritual," I replied. "I'm more into earthly practicalities."

"You're bullshitting yourself," Dan retorted. "Don't you remember when we came over the Indian River Bridge, where you can see the ocean? I saw you following the horizon as far as you could, and I heard you sigh. I bet that view inspires you every time you go over that bridge. That's God at work."

"Why can't it just be the freedom of my own human mind to find beauty, even amongst ugliness, without equating either to the presence of God?" I asked before changing the subject. This guy is pretty intuitive, I thought. Indeed, I love that view.

"So you said you were different from your Dad."

"Yeah, I'm much more like my Mom. She is a dreamer, artistic, and gentle."

I wanted to delve into his past, to validate the pain I heard in his voice, saw in the tightening of his hands as he spoke. But it didn't seem to be my business, so once more I brought the conversation to safe ground.

"Where did you go to high school?" I asked.

"You wouldn't know it – it's a small private school, very elite."

"Try me," I said. He told me its name.

"I know it," I responded triumphantly. "The school I attended for a year when I first came to America played baseball against yours! I was sixteen, an English kid in an enclave of diplomats' precocious sons and daughters."

Flashbacks of teenage privilege danced through my memory. Like with Jean Paul from France when he drove me for my first visit to a Hot Shoppes restaurant and ordered a "Mighty Mo and a chocolate shake" on a loud speaker. It was served by a girl whizzing around on roller skates.

With Karin from Denmark, I screamed support for our school football team. With Terence from Burma, I crashed my first embassy party. With Judy from England, I visited residents of a home for the blind in Georgetown every Saturday morning. With everyone in the school, I knelt against the assembly room wall with my head buried in my arms practicing for the eventuality of a cold war nuclear blast. With Robin as my date, I danced as princess at our senior prom.

My year in this high school gave me a little taste of background to understand Dan. He is one of society's privileged few who grow up in a world of affluence and with the best of education. Not from the super-rich but the offspring of parents and grandparents who have struggled for what they have achieved in America. They are proud of their lineage and place high value on their children's scholastic successes. Dan is like many of the kids I went to school with, their reality so narrow that they think their lives are the norm.

"That's weird. I hardly ever meet someone who knows of either of those schools."

"What about college?" I asked.

He mentioned the name of the prestigious university he had loved but not graduated from. His major had been English. I mentally calculated his age and realized he was older than could be accounted from years in school.

Checking for inconsistencies in a person's history was an automatic thing for me to do. I must have reviewed close to a thousand résumé's over the years, selecting hundreds of candidates to interview. There might be valid reasons for excluding blocks of time, but usually they represent periods a person wishes to forget yet knows better than to lie about.

"There are gaps in your story," I challenged. "They're your business but often it's those things one doesn't talk about that provide the best fodder for writing." I wanted to ask more but I was sure he would tell me in time.

He looked at me thoughtfully. This time was his turn to change the topic.

"What about you? I don't know anything about you either."

* * *

My book of poems caused Dan and I to meet. Writing poems was our bond. Poetry is the vehicle we both use to think through what is going on in our lives. It is easier for us to express our thoughts and feelings first in writing and then use those words as the basis to discuss whatever was on our minds. Poetry absorbed much of our driving-in-the-car-time chitter-chatter. Poetry and music.

The next time Dan got in the car, he asked if he could turn on the radio, something I almost never do. It's part of my Parkinson's, this need to concentrate on one thing at a time, like driving. Just thinking while driving was enough of a distraction.

My mind was always going a mile a minute, just over the speed limit. The last thing I needed was for both my thinking and driving to be influenced by the radio. I used to spend my time while at the wheel listening to books on tape or to the endless stream of voicemail messages while remaining focused on safety. Those were the good old days.

"Sure," I said. "Pick the station." He did, oldies but goodies that first time. We sang along and laughed and felt the rhythm. Music became habit when he was in the car. Occasionally, when he would turn to a station he thought I wouldn't like, I surprised him by knowing and liking Janis Joplin, Jimi Hendrix, and Dan's two favorites, Bob Marley and John Lennon.

Dan referenced lines from their works in his poems and short stories, and he would quote himself as we drove along. One quote led to another, interlaced with discussion. Between singer songwriters, he would interject the words of others like his favorite author, Jack Kerouac.

Dan's side of the conversation sounded something like this: "Could Bob Marley have been right when he sang about the people of the world really loving each other 'in peace and harmony, instead of fear, fussing and fighting, like we ain't supposed to be?' No, no. That's just a slogan, we can't take his brilliance literally, it wouldn't work."

Or, "Take the words from Lennon's famous song, *Imagine*. Critics have said they are amongst the finest lyrics ever written. I'm not the only dreamer, you know. Yet we just sing along and then stack the meaning in a file cabinet without doing anything. Its no wonder European kids look down their noses at us Americans. They make their voices known."

With each twang of the guitar beat, each new quote, a day of Parkinson's stiffness seemed to ease away. In his presence, I felt younger, vibrant, interesting. To someone whose middle years are being nibbled away, that reality cannot be overstated.

"By the way, I've got to see my doctor tomorrow, I'm in a Parkinson's research program, but the next day I'm having another book signing," I mentioned as I dropped him off.

"It's at the same place we were today, at seven in the evening. This time I'll also be reading some of my poems and displaying my pictures. You can come if you want."

* * *

The year following my admission into the life-long research study, I was asked to participate in another. This one focused on the daily lives of Parkinson's patients and their care givers. Between the two studies and the visits to various psychiatrists, including Dr. Leo, Ike and I were up and down the state of Delaware about six times each year. It became a familiar journey.

One of the psychiatrists assigned to me at the medical center was a kind and gentle man who listened well and spoke softly. I liked and trusted him. He and his wife are Korean by birth and he had proudly talked to me about the birth of his son and the meaning of the boy's Korean name. He lent me photos from which I made a collage. "I had it framed and it sits on the table in our hallway," he told me. I felt comfortable to email him on a couple of occasions when my life seemed to be getting out of control. He always responded quickly.

"How are you doing?" he asked, as usual.

I told him about the success I was having with my *Delaware* book and gave him a signed copy. Then I told him about the luncheon and I read him the entirety of my *Shells of Themselves* poem. He nodded sympathetically and asked if there was anything else.

"Well I've met a young writer whom I've taken under my wing," I said.

"That's good. You seem to find strength in helping people. Use your writing and your photos to make a difference in others' lives."

Then he gave me a prescription for a different anti-depressant to add to my Parkinson's cocktail.

* * *

The book signing was important to me. I enjoyed public speaking since my childhood. That was a time of elocution lessons and competitions at the town hall. My certificates of success were buried somewhere in the depth of an old orange steamer trunk where I keep all my mementos. The trunk had once belonged to a congressman and was given me by an old boyfriend. Ike and I had painted it to match the seventies orange and brown decor of our first house. I hoped the busy bookshop environment wouldn't distract me. I practiced on Ike until I could tell I was close to the line.

Ike is a patient man, having dealt with decades of red tape trying to provide the best services for his way-under-privileged clients. But having a new poem thrust in his face while sitting on the toilet each morning, was a tad more than even he was prepared for. We often remind each other that a rose garden was not among our promises.

By the time we arrived at the bookshop many of the seats placed in rows in front of the podium had already been taken. Around the periphery of the group several friends helped me arrange the framed photographs that corresponded with the poems. I was excited yet comfortable in the familiar surroundings of the bookshop and the well-wishers. I was pleased with my book and loved to read from it. There was more a sense of accomplishment than pride. I'd started and finished something.

Before reading my first poem I looked out at the audience of many recently-made friends and said, "I'd like to recognize my husband and my best friend, Ike. It is because of him I have been able to ride my wave of change." He looked around from his seat and grinned meekly at the warm applause.

Dan arrived, punctual as ever. I noticed him right away and smiled in acknowledgement of his inconspicuous wave. He was one of just a few twenty-somethings in an audience whose average age was around fifty. During the break, I introduced him to Ike and they chatted briefly.

Signing my books and sipping wine at the end of the evening, I glowed with pride. When I stopped at the bookshop the following day for my cup of café mocha, the hard-working manager greeted me. "It was the best full day we've ever had. I couldn't believe the register and re-counted all the receipts!" he exalted. My glow evolved to a neon beam.

For the first time since moving to Bethany, I felt really well.

5

A Good Listener Meets a Good Liar

"I'm going kayaking. Do you want to come?" It was a new friend's voice on the line.

"I'd love to but I've never done it before. When?" It was an unhesitating answer. My recent, major back surgery never crossed my mind. With my book's success and Dan's presence, the summer was becoming a serendipitous whirlwind of spur of the moment adventure.

"Guess what?" I said to Dan on the way up to the next Writers' Cabin meeting. "I'm going kayaking this afternoon. I've never been before and I'm excited."

"Cool. I've never kayaked either. Guess what's funny, too?" he continued. "I dreamed about Morgan Freeman last night, but I think it was really Ike! There was this girl in my dream too. She was trying to decide whether to come after me or Morgan."

"Morgan Freeman? The one from *Driving Miss Daisy*?"

"The very one. I liked that movie. You?"

"Sure," I said. In fact I was starting to dislike the movie, or at least what it represented. Ike sometimes refers to me as Miss Daisy because I occasionally lie on the back seat while he is driving: the combination of Parkinson's and a bad back makes lying more comfortable and I often nod off as he chauffeurs me along.

Being likened to Miss Daisy is the kind of subtle sidebar message that makes me think that I am closer to being old like Jessica Tandy than Ike is to Morgan Freeman. And now the idea of Ike being in Dan's lusty dream did nothing to heighten the appeal of the movie! I explained some of this to Dan and was surprised he understood my sensitivity.

"Don't worry, I'll just call you Miss Christina," he kidded, just like Dad would have. "But do take care of your back in that kayak."

Uh oh, now Dan was on the "take care of" kick too!

* * *

Dan participated readily at the Cabin meeting. He liked the description by one of the planning meeting members, "A place for writers to find their voice."

As we drove back, I decided I needed to know more about Dan's person before he got carried away finding his voice. His life was starting to become my business. So I asked, and the words came tumbling forth, unencumbered by the restraint that might normally exist between two people who only knew each other about a week.

He'd started taking drugs when his girlfriend left him after his sophomore year in college. "I was devastated. I loved her." His recreational joint became a daily habit. Then he dropped some acid, did a little cocaine, "my dope of choice", and escalated to heroin. At first he kept up with his schoolwork, but then flunked out the following semester.

"My parents sent me to a great program," he told me. "You've probably heard of it, but I left before they thought I was ready."

Dan described that rehabilitation program as being spiritual. It was based on the twelve-step recovery process that forms the basis for the Alcoholic Anonymous and related dependency programs. Like almost all alcohol and drug programs, it preaches total abstinence and regular attendance at AA or Narcotics Anonymous meetings.

Dan told me that he didn't like the absolute black and white of this philosophy. He wanted to keep open the possibility that he could some day become an occasional user without being addicted. After leaving the program Dan stayed clean for thirty days before starting to use again. His parents remained unaware of his relapse for some time.

"I guess you'd say I was a functioning addict. I had three part-time jobs: babysitting, coaching baseball, and working in a friend's store. I lived at home, always ate well and kept fit, and had lots of friends. Most of my crowd was like me; their parents had money, trusted their kids and everyone did a little weed or whatever. Life was fun except my friends all stayed in school and got good jobs and I stayed high."

"I thought you said you babysat?"

"Well that's when the problems started. First I'd just use in the evening, and then I might have a quick hit before the day started. And then things started to get real heavy again. Soon it was out of hand. But I never put the kids at risk. I love kids."

"What happened then?"

"One of my friends turned me in to my Dad. I couldn't believe it. Betrayed me without telling me first what he was going to do. I lost everything immediately, my jobs, money which I spent on drugs anyway. I couldn't leave the house, see any of my friends. The guy I worked for kept calling because I'd stolen money from the till. My Dad looked like he could kill me with disappointment. My Mom kept hugging me and telling me it would be all right. She's so protective. It was awful."

I couldn't imagine what his parents had gone through. Of course, I'd heard of these situations before but always second hand. Dan was my kids' generation. Raised in Washington's suburbs, they were both certainly exposed to excess, and probably tempted fate more than I ever hope to know. But Dan's level of addiction was a different class of problem and I was hearing it directly from his mouth.

He told me I was the first person he voiced some of this to and once he got started the story flowed.

"My Dad found out about this other rehab program. He got talked into it, the total opposite of the first place. It was inner city and was filled with hard core addicts, all black. I was the only white boy, the only one with any college education. That didn't bother me. A good friend in high school was black. But these were ghetto guys. Most of them had spent time in jail. For them, this place was better than jail or the streets. For some, it was even better than being at home."

"Every day they told me I'd end up in jail too. It really got to me, so I would bait some of them, just enough that they would get right up close to me. But we all knew the non-negotiable consequence of fighting, so they backed down. I just tried to mind my own business and write. But, except for a couple of guys, I hated it there. I convinced my parents I had to leave. I smoked a joint within fifteen minutes of leaving. My parents let me come here to sort things out. They think I'm still clean. I'm a really good liar."

"Yeah," Dan repeated softly, looking me in the eye, "I'm a really good liar."

I heard it as a warning. I just listened and absorbed.

He reached into his book bag and extracted a small spiral notebook and read one of the poems he had written in the facility he hated so much. He yearned to escape its reality by sneaking back to bed and escaping to *"the solace of sleep."* It ends: *"I get high sleeping, Tonight will be my 37th night, Sweet dreams."*

I wasn't surprised that Dan was a drug user but I didn't expect the depth of the problem. I knew his prognosis was dim, especially as he left two programs prematurely. Nevertheless, it never occurred to me to tell him that his addiction precluded our continuing relationship, whatever that might mean.

His warning to me that he was an expert liar rang true. I felt that he wanted to be honest with me and he understood that I would be nothing but honest with him. I recognized there was a fine line between open mindedness and naïveté, but I thought helping Dan with his writing, might just be what he needed to get his life together.

In my Wave of Change poem, I described myself as *"a spirit, now freed to be flawed"* after being *"constrained by years of doing things right, controlled to conform to the norm."* I liked my expression about it being okay not to be perfect all the time. I consciously told myself that this was the time to wear my non-judgmental hat while removing all rose-colored tint from my spectacles.

I told Dan that Ike and I had both worked in hospitals and, specifically of Ike's professional background, as a psychiatric social worker. I preached that in our house and in my presence he must never use drugs. He nodded in agreement.

Dan and I agreed that he would come to the house the next day so he could share some more of his writing. I wanted to see whether he had what it took to be accepted at the Writers' Cabin, should it become a reality. We ended our conversation with a high five. I noted with satisfaction that I was becoming quite adept with high fives.

* * *

The conversation reminded me of the years our next door neighbor both smoked and grew marijuana. I used to be so concerned that a seed or two from the tall weeds that rose above the garden fence would somehow take root in our own back yard, contaminating our tomatoes. Our neighbor had his own problems with the law relating to sharing his homegrown product with willing friends.

Ike and I joined him and his sons at a meeting with a lawyer to help think his court room strategy through. Ike and I were a team back then, helping others. I really thought we could be a helping team again.

Yet, I was glad not to see Ike's car in the driveway as I turned onto our street. The news about Dan's drug addiction had been disconcerting, and I wasn't ready to share it. Addiction was an understood problem in both our families – alcohol, as well as drugs.

Ike's connection with drugs extended to his professional capacity through his patients. I remember several occasions when he escorted youngsters back across the country to grief-stricken parents. These kids came to the Nation's Capitol for fun and excitement, but left with their minds damaged by angel dust and ecstasy.

Our marriage has always been based on open communication and a shared sense of humor. It wasn't a question of not telling him the latest news about my new friend but just one of how and when.

* * *

I waited until Ike finished reading the newspaper the next day and drank his obligatory two cups of coffee, before bringing up the subject of Dan.

"You remember he came to the Writers' Cabin meeting with me yesterday? Well, he is really interested in it and it could be a way for him to get grounded, and focus on writing."

"So?"

"He has problems, Ike: drugs, two rehab efforts, and still using grass. He just may be ready to change and maybe I can help him with his writing."

"A leopard doesn't change its spots. How do you know all this?"

"He told me on the way back from the meeting. I asked him to come over later today so I could see more of his writing. I want to make sure that I think it is good or else I'm wasting both of our time."

"Why are you getting involved? He's got parents, doesn't he? I don't like it." He turned his back to me and took his time putting on his outside tennis shoes. "Bungy!" He called our dog, clicked her lead, got a blue pooper-scooper bag and departed, following Bungy's wagging tail and springing step. Not another word had passed between us.

The intensity of Ike's reaction surprised me. We have supported people with problems before. I felt a defensive shield rising to cover my vulnerability. My motivation to befriend Dan was being questioned, and I resented the implication.

* * *

Dan came over that afternoon. Ike was in the kitchen and the three of us chatted for a while until Dan and I went up to my studio and Ike went to his workbench in the garage. I read Dan some of my poems and he said the right things about my photos. He read me some of his work, we talked about it and then he started to type into an old laptop I decided to lend him. I liked the irony in his writing, but was saddened by its pessimism.

Our dialog was open, intense and challenging. I told him "You're giving up your control over your own mind to a chemical that makes you feel good. Your writing is as free flowing as your mind on weed. It needs discipline, like you do!"

"Yeah but –" He hesitated, knowing there was no answer that would satisfy me. He saw I wouldn't stand for old arguments about government clandestinely sanctioning drug imports.

"You may or not be right about that," I told him. "But so what? The big picture is irrelevant to your need to focus on you. Try to write about your own experiences. Something concrete, that people can relate to."

"I know you won't," Dan said, "but you should try marijuana some time. Your poems are good but a touch more imagination, a whiff of the unknown..." He stopped his tease mid-sentence with a raise of his eyebrow, and a toast with his can of orange soda.

I had forgotten how much I missed just talking and debating about words, feelings, religion, and silly things, too. Those trans-Atlantic phone calls with Dad, the on-the-road dinner table discussions with my work colleagues, even just casual chats about nothing with Greg, all seemed distant memories.

We put aside talk of Dan's personal issues and had fun, exercising our minds with words and poems. We took turns starting with a line and then the other would add a couple more. We allowed our thoughts to lead us, competing with each other on vocabulary. Most were silly and some were really funny.

The last poem started with a dark cloud looming on the horizon. It continued with the fear of a family hearing wind rushing down the railway track, then a demolished home, a little girl's missing father, and the poignancy of Dan's last line, "Daddy, you promised you'd never leave me."

The afternoon flew by, reminding me of when my Dad and I would banter on the correct usage of a word. How I missed my ageless Dad and his words of wisdom. It was refreshing to exchange barbs and share wit.

* * *

When we went downstairs, Dan noted that Ike was washing his car.

"May I help?" he asked. "Believe it or not I've never washed a car before and I heard of this place that might add car washing to its line of services. You know I need to make some money. Would you teach me?" Together, they washed and polished both our cars. Poor little rich kid, I thought.

"I always take care of my car, give it a bath each week," I heard Ike say. "This is the first car I ever was able to buy new and I want it to look good for a long time." Later he cautioned, "Don't forget to put the lid on the polish and put away your rag. You've got to look after your tools."

Ike seemed open to Dan's company so I cautiously added a place for him at the supper table. Dan knew that I already told Ike about his addiction and I was aware that Ike was paying close attention to Dan while we ate our typical

Friday fish supper, Southern style corn meal-breaded and fried, with our fingers. We keep a grease container next to the stove for the run off from the likes of cooking bacon and use it to fry fish, chicken and potatoes. It was a new way of dining for Dan. He was relaxed and enjoying himself. Ironic, I suppose, to be so concerned about the effect of weed on Dan's health while the mere smell from our stove was enough to clog our own arteries!

Then, out of the blue, Ike said what was on his mind: "I've worked with addicts for thirty-seven years. Alcohol and drug abuse is in my family. I expect you have stolen, probably even from those you love the most. All addicts will do whatever they need to do and you've probably done it all. This I tell you and I tell you once, never lie to me or you can forget having anything to do with me."

The mood around the table darkened. Dan looked subdued and asked Ike what his work was like. He listened carefully as Ike expounded. "Well, I worked with in-patients first, on the wards. You had to have at least one man on duty in case anyone went crazy. I did it all, gave them their medications, helped keep them clean and fed, and I did a lot of observing and listening. I got to be a good listener and a pretty good judge of character. Well, you have to be when you're looking out for your hind parts. I got injured a few times and disappointed plenty more. After I got my degree, I moved into community mental health. I tried to get my patients a place to live, enough money for food, all the things that are an additional burden to them on top of their head problems. Listening and observing, those are the big things, though."

The conversation led to Ike telling a couple of funny Saint Elizabeth's stories and the mood lightened up again. It didn't take long for us to be laughing about Ike's latest fishing antics and shared opinions about the Washington

Redskins' upcoming season. Love of the 'Skins was one thing Ike and Dan had in common. Like the weather, fishing and football were the stuff of easy dialog.

"Hey, I'll wash the dishes, you can dry," Dan said as naturally as if he were part of the family.

After we cleaned up together, I put on my old LP of the Beatles: *Sergeant Pepper's Lonely Heart's Club Band*. Dan knew almost all the songs, and at times all three of us were in full voice. I sang happily with such verses as *"Will you still feed me, will you still need me, when I'm sixty-four?"* I was a bit taken aback to see Dan's bemused glance when I sang *"Lucy in the Sky with diamonds."* I had forgotten the song was alluding to LSD. So, then I put on good old John Denver, one of my all time favorites. Suddenly Dan and I were singing an awesome rendition of *"Poems, prayers and promises, and thing that we believe in – and pass the pipe around!"*

Then it was time for him to go. He now had both the backpack and the heavy old computer to carry. "Would you mind if Dan borrowed the extra bike?" I asked Ike.

He looked at me as though I had lost my mind. "You better look after it. Here's the padlock and key," he mumbled.

Dan rode off on the bike with the backpack pulling him sideways and the computer attached with a bungy cord. He looked off balance. I was reminded of the last person to use the bike – Dad on his final visit. He had fallen off and had sat dejected on the ground as a neighbor came to tell us. He told the ER doctor that riding a bike was another of those things he'd never do again. Such a damned shame he fell off. He died back in England three months later.

The phone rang in about fifteen minutes.

"I had a great day," Dan said, "The best for a long time. I love being at your house. I don't think I've ever been around such a non-dysfunctional couple before. I really like Ike. He's so down to earth. You know exactly where he's coming from."

I suppose Dan had picked up that sense of family normalcy when he called Ike and me non-dysfunctional. Non-dysfunctional, I thought to myself. I don't know about that. Our marriage has its share of ups and downs, but we've always gotten off the seesaw on level ground.

But life since retirement was more difficult. The proximity of togetherness emphasized our differences. Ike likes TV. My computer is my best friend. I get up before six, often before four; he arises around nine. He needs routine and I love spontaneity. He enjoys privacy. I share my soul.

My Parkinson's was also a cause of unease. Ike's promise to my Dad that he would take care of me had caused a premature protectiveness that irritated me. I resented the need to be looked after. I think I know when I need help, and I ask for it. Being constantly reminded to check the car for gas or to not drive too far made me feel feeble. I was difficult to live with. Ike and I were becoming disturbingly distant. It was uncomfortable but we were stuck in the mind-set "ignore it and it will get better."

What never waivers in our relationship are the fundamentals. Race has never been an issue for either of us. Other people may have a problem but we have never let theirs become ours. Our decision to have children cemented our marriage. Children of mixed racial relationships already have an added dimension to their lives. They don't need the burden of instability at home as well.

Our politics are another shared value. We refuse to allow the country's right wing to demean the word "liberal". Neither of us espouses organized religion or even a conventional belief in God. I just don't get the need. Because we don't go to church, it occurred to us early in our marriage that we needed to establish our own little nuclear family traditions for the major religious holidays. Every Christmas after the kids opened their presents, we drove to the site of the national Christmas tree, south of the White House, and no matter how cold the weather, we would walk around the circle of trees decorated by children from each state. Then we'd warm up by going to ooh and ah at the magnificent displays of poinsettias at the Botanical Gardens near the Capitol. On Easter, we'd go for a picnic at the National Arboretum. Sometimes the daffodils, my favorite flowers, in fern valley would still be in bloom; usually the dogwoods would have spread their pink and white blossoms on spindly branches like a field of open umbrellas. Ike taught me how to drive my first car, a VW bug, in the Arboretum and Greg and Kim both learned to ride their bikes there. It is our place of peace.

Finally we share a sense of humor. Thus far, we have always looked for and found something to laugh about, although recently only just in time.

I'm not sure why I decided to tell Kim and Greg about Dan. Perhaps I hoped they would understand my desire to be able to help someone. I know I hoped they would relate to a person more their age and help ease things between Ike and me.

I wanted them to know and like Dan. I wanted my friend to become theirs. It wasn't their concern, yet I've always shared my life with them, and Dan was in my life. I was enjoying his presence, but not in a way that required secrecy.

I told them on the phone, separately, about meeting him at the book signing, his love of writing and his use of marijuana (but not his addiction to heroin). Greg responded that I'd be surprised how many young people smoke a joint. As long as he didn't do drugs around me, I should mind my own business about it and focus on his writing. After all, Greg noted, look at how many of the best authors and artists smoked pot. "But," he cautioned, "don't let him be alone in the house."

Kim's reaction was different. She was in tune with my conscience. "Mom, you mustn't do anything that Dad doesn't want you to do. With something like this, you really have to work as partners. I worry about you."

"Of course, I'll work with Dad. That's why I'm being so open about this, why I'm letting you know." I didn't like my tone. I was cross with myself for having caused her concern. Were our roles starting to reverse? Surely not yet.

6

Caught

I expected to hear from Dan again by the next writing group meeting, but there was no word so I went alone. Billy was the only one there. He was depressed. Instead of reading our stuff we luxuriated in shared misery.

Dan's sudden absence was on my mind. I was annoyed that he would disappear without saying farewell, and worried that something was wrong. I imagined him alone in the condo dying from an overdose, or suicide. Or perhaps he was involved with some girl. That would be the best reason.

And what about Ike's bike? Ike pointed to the empty space along the wall in the garage several times as if to say, "I told you so." Heck, why not admit it? I was depressed too. I kept thinking about the word "depression" as I drove home. When I got there Ike was engrossed in TV. Once again, I went straight upstairs and sat in front of my computer. Those are the moments when I'm driven to write, not by hand, I can't read my own scribble now.

I finished a poem and read it aloud to myself, as I always do. I realized I had taken the topic to a much greater depth than I was feeling myself. I felt pleased that in my writing, I was able to get outside my own level of experience:

> *It can strike*
> *Without warning*
> *Like the smack of*
> *Cold*

Christina Weaver

When the
Morgue
Door
Opens wide,
Inviting

Sometimes
It creeps in
Like a parasite
Worming
Through the bowel
Metastasizing
Chemical imbalance
Until it
Settles, malignant
In the crevices
Of the mind

Mostly
It's always
There
Just hidden
Better
Some days
Than others
Concealed
By a
Smile
Cocooned in
Camouflage

I printed it and took it in the living room to show Ike.

"Hey, look, what do you think? It's about depression, which is a downer, but what about the way I've written it?"

"Can't you see I'm watching my show?" he replied. "After this comes *Law and Order*. I'll look at it after that. It'll still be around tomorrow, won't it? You have to have everything done NOW."

The poem went back upstairs with me. I should have known better. "That damn Dan," I thought, "why isn't he around to share this with me? I need to share it with someone."

Five days after Dan borrowed the bike, I heard Ike answer the phone. "Oh, we wondered where you had gone. Back home for a couple of days, I see. So, you're all right? Good. Hang on. Phone!" he yelled.

I took the portable from him and went upstairs, to be by myself. "I expect you wondered where I've been." Dan's voice was low and in monotone. The kind of voice you have to sit down to listen to.

"I got arrested," he said.

I didn't know what to say.

"Where? When? How?" I spat out.

"Intent to distribute marijuana, ugh, on the boardwalk, ugh, trying to run away, ugh, assaulting an officer, ugh, but I didn't..."

Pause.

"This is the first time I've ever been fucking arrested, ever, I swear."

"So you didn't go home?"

Pause.

I felt sick that he'd lied and sad that he had confirmed the addict stereotype. My organizing defense system rushed forward.

"What about your parents? Do you have a lawyer? When is the trial? Have you eaten anything?"

"I've pretty much just been in bed," he said. Since getting out of jail the day following the arrest, Dan had done little but seek solace under the bed covers, once again escaping reality by sleeping.

"You'd better come over," I told him. "Ride the bike."

Unfortunately, the safety of Ike's bike hadn't been high on Dan's mind on the evening of his bust. He'd forgotten the lock. When he got out of jail and the police officer drove him back to the center of Bethany where he had parked the bike, it was gone. I was silent as only middle-class English women and American Episcopalians can be. Even more than the arrest, the bike would put Ike over the top. He was so careful about his possessions and rarely threw anything away.

"Well just get over here," I demanded. I thought it would serve him right to walk the half mile to our house. He arrived within minutes, riding a decidedly fancier bike.

"Where in the world did this bike come from?" The shrug and a few brief words indicated that it had been substituted from a bike rank in the same manner Ike's was taken.

"It's stolen?" I ranted. "You've come over here on a stolen bike? What if it's been reported as stolen and the police stopped you? You'd be in even greater trouble."

He parked the bike around the corner from the house so Ike wouldn't see it and got in the car. We drove to a quiet place where we wouldn't be interrupted. He mumbled, I yelled.

"Oh, that's just great, whatever the actual truth, they wouldn't have arrested you for nothing. I just can't believe that one afternoon we are playing word games and the next evening you're this damned stupid, in this town that I love. You are an addict all right, just thinking of you and the next fix. Hell with the consequences, your parents, me."

"This is the bottom," he said. "I have touched the low point in my life. Those kids in the last treatment center taunted me saying I would go to prison and they were right. My parents can't know, they just couldn't take it, especially my Dad. I'm quitting for good. I really mean it. Seventy-two hours clean already. That job called and I'm starting next week. God, what a fucking fool I am."

"But what about the arrest? What happens next?"

He pulled out a crumpled summons telling him to be at the county courthouse the next day.

My tirade continued, "Tomorrow? How are you getting there? On a stolen bike? Who's your lawyer? Don't you know how serious this is? This is a felony. They could lock you up tomorrow. You're a danger to the community."

Eyes cast down, shoulders hunched, his words came, slow and subdued. "It was just marijuana. I didn't have any money on me. I've never been arrested for anything before. I'll hitchhike there. Such a fucking fool."

"Such a fucking fool, all right." I agreed. But I wasn't clear which of us I was talking about. I took him back to his place and told him to stay there, and check the yellow pages for lawyers and local treatment programs. I told him that I would go with him the next day. Nobody should go to court alone.

"Thank you." Instead of a high five, he gave me a quick hug, one human being to another. As he turned away, I called his name.

"By the way, do you remember who arrested you?"

He told me the officer's name and described each one he had met. There was the tall one who stopped him, the muscular one who laughed at him in handcuffs, and the young one who said, "I wished we had met under other circumstances."

I decided to go past the police station to get some advice. My mother's repetition of the old admonition about "if you need help, ask a policeman" was firmly entrenched.

Recognizing an officer in the lobby, I said: "May I ask you something? Someone, a young man I met but don't know well, was arrested by one of your colleagues – for trying to sell marijuana. I'm really grateful he was arrested. It was the best thing that could have happened. I'm so annoyed with him, and I'm trying to decide what to do, what role to take. If this were someone you knew, what would you do? What would you do if he was your family member?"

"I know what you're talking about. It's a good case. Don't tell me anything I don't know. But if I were you, the best thing you can do is to make sure he has a good lawyer." The officer, not much older than Dan, proceeded to give me the names of the two he considered best. I again felt glad we had moved somewhere where I could feel comfortable asking an officer for advice.

I was sad for Dan, and angry with him. I was sad for myself – no longer would he be "my friend in writing" instead "my young friend, the addict."

* * *

"So you think you can save him." Ike oozed sarcasm. I had told him about the arrest and going to court the next day. I didn't mention the bicycle.

"I'm not going to court with him to save him. I just don't think he should go off to court by himself. I plan to help him understand he has to confide in his parents. I know he's his own responsibility first and theirs next, but somehow I'm in the middle of it and I want to see this piece through."

"It's your business, not mine." Ike turned away, his back was poker stiff, his shoulders squared. He knew there was no point in telling me to get uninvolved.

The phone rang. "Oh, it's you." Ike handed me the portable as though it were contaminated.

I went upstairs. Dan had made an appointment to see a defense lawyer early in the morning. It wasn't one of the names the officer gave me but I was pleased that he showed the initiative to follow through.

"I'll walk over and get the bike," he suggested.

"No, that's the last thing we need, for you to have that bike in your possession. I'll think about what we need to do. It can't stay where it is."

"Ike really hates me doesn't he? Is there anything I can say to him, anything to change his mind?"

"No, not yet. He'll come around." I still thought he would.

* * *

The bicycle became a symbol of the difference in our consciences. To Dan, it was an inconsequential sideline of a much bigger problem. For me, it was a warning. There are perils in becoming too close to one with an impaired sense of morality. In retrospect, it had me teetering on the edge of enabling.

The greater philosophic issues of right and wrong took a backseat to the practicality of getting rid of the damn bike. I hid it in our garage overnight, and planned to put it back where Dan had taken it from the next day. There was no need to set an alarm as I was always awake by five.

I woke up thinking about the bike first and going to court second. It made a change to have something to do, other than going to my computer. I slid quietly from under the sheets and got dressed without Ike's noticing my absence. Bungy, our old gray cockapoo helped me, moving her body next to his, so Ike remained cozy under the covers.

Afraid that opening the garage doors might disturb Ike, I carefully wheeled the bike through the kitchen and out the front door. It was bigger than I expected, and hard to maneuver. I opened the car trunk and realized it was already half full with my normal accumulation of picture frames, beach chairs and blankets. One last item remained when one of our development's security guards drove by.

"Nice morning," he said, glad to have someone to talk to at the end of his long and oh so routine, night shift. "You're up early. Tell Ike that the fish should be jumping this afternoon. Oh, and do you need any help?"

"No, no. I'm fine, just moving some things around," I assured him. I watched him drive back up the street and turn the corner.

With all my strength, I lifted the bike and shoved it into the trunk. It wouldn't go. I re-angled it and the back half got wedged. I used a bungy cord to prevent the front wheel from whizzing around and set off slowly, down the street, around the corner, and across the highway.

My luck held. Nobody was around. Looking from side to side I backed up to the bike rack of the large, ground level garage. Leaving the engine running, I released the bungy cord and tugged at the bike as hard as I could. It wouldn't budge.

Perspiration haloed my hair line and drenched my armpits. I felt the pulse in my temple race as I wiped away sweat. With my adrenalin in overdrive I got it with the next pull. I scratched the car – small matter. I stood the bike by the rack, leaning it against another unchained temptation.

In the car again, I shifted into drive. Oh my God, I thought suddenly, my fingerprints are all over the bike. I put the car back into neutral, and pulled on the handbrake. I was wearing a new National Wildlife tee shirt blooming with hummingbirds and wild flowers. Fortunately, it was a Large. I stuck my hand under it and wiped off the handlebars and fenders. I looked as dirty as I felt but I couldn't resist a giggle to myself at the incongruity of the moment.

At home I stood in the shower a long time. I shampooed my hair and shaved my legs and under my arms. With my focus now on going to court, I still felt dirty.

* * *

I had driven to Georgetown, the Sussex County seat, a couple of weeks before. It was to give copies of my book to the officials in the Small Business division who had been so helpful and encouraged me to publish it. One of the photos in the book is of the nineteenth century stocks sitting in the square by the courthouse. Maybe it would serve Dan right to be placed in the stocks and jeered at for a few days. Ike would have been certain to chuck a couple of rotten tomatoes at him, eggs to boot! I wonder if a little certain public humiliation would serve as a better deterrent than the possibility of prison these days.

Dan didn't ask about the bike, but I told him about my antics of the early morn. I described the scenario as a slapstick comedy with a hint of a lesson in morality.

He laughed. "I think you'd better turn yourself in," he teased.

The sun shone in a cloudless sky foretelling the heat of midday. I'd taken one of Ike's ties before I left the house. It was navy blue with little white peace doves that I thought best fit the occasion. Ike wears it to funerals. Dan tied it under the collar of his short sleeve white shirt. "Nice," he commented, as he checked his appearance in the visor mirror.

First, we went to Dan's lawyer. Dan went into the conference room. They shut the door. After about ten minutes, his head appeared around the corner.

"Would you come on in? I need someone else to listen with me and think what to ask." The lawyer introduced himself and asked, "Now exactly how do you fit in to all this?"

"Well, it is rather strange. I've known him less than three weeks. We met because I was having a book signing and Dan showed interest. He told me he smoked grass but this arrest business was much more than I ever expected. In fact, I've met several of the Bethany police officers and thanked them for making the arrest. I don't want pushers in my town, period. Indeed I'm glad he was arrested. Maybe this will be what it takes to get him to normal behavior."

The lawyer looked at me for a moment before saying, "That's very nice of you to help him." It was as though my niceness was more abnormal than Dan's predicament.

Then he explained Delaware's laws governing drug use and selling. "The citizens have indicated their lack of tolerance for drug offences. Judges do not want to be considered soft on this matter. If you are found guilty, you will do time in prison as a felon."

It was a sobering discussion. Then the lawyer explained his strategy for dealing with the case. He planned to request postponement. It was essential that Dan stay clean from then on. Marijuana stays in the urine for as long as six weeks and he would be tested in court on the day of the trial.

"Don't waste my time and your life by using again," he said.

As we were leaving it occurred to me to ask for the home address Dan had given the police. His face turned pallid. His hands held his head and he paced. His parents' address was on his driver's license. Court notices might have already been sent to his home. What a terrible way for his parents to discover he had let them down again.

"They just couldn't deal with it. I've put them through hell already. My Dad, he mustn't find out."

Quickly, the secretary checked at the courthouse. No notices had been sent out yet. Dan raised his arms, hands clenched, in relief. "Yes!" He looked at me, and without the question being asked, I nodded. The secretary changed his address to ours.

"Ike's going to be thrilled with this development," I muttered.

Dan looked down. His world was falling apart. He'd been to two rehab centers and wasn't able to stay clean. Could he do it now? He must do it now. He laid his forehead on the table between his elbows. I noticed two small, circular, ugly open sores on the underside of his left wrist and made a mental note to ask about them later.

* * *

We walked in stifling heat to the courthouse. After queuing outside to get through the metal detector, we spent hours waiting for Dan's name to be called. An endless succession of wretched people took their turn before the judge. We guessed who would walk to the exit, grinning, and who would be handcuffed and led away, face averted. Dan pulled out one of his notebooks and we played HANGMAN!

At one point, I found myself putting a hand out to comfort the mother of an alleged teenage rapist. Dan had talked to her son while they were waiting to meet the public defender and had told me the guy said the girl had made it up. Apparently, the judge thought so, too, as mother and son left the courtroom smiling, arm in arm. She turned her head towards Dan and me as they walked past us, as though to say, "good luck."

I was relieved when they left.

I had a flashback of my own rape that awful day in the laundry room of the apartment where we lived when we were first married. Two young men had followed me. The door hadn't locked properly. I tried to escape but was no match for the belt that was slipped around my neck. "Give us some pussy, bitch," one said. I remember the heart with an arrow and two names painted in red on the cinder block wall as I lay on the concrete floor next to the drain. I remember the arrogant intern in the emergency room who implied it was my fault for living in SE Washington, DC. In my mind he was the third rapist, the one who raped my soul.

I was lucky, in a way. When I ran from the laundry room to the resident manager's office, I tripped and broke a toe. It swelled up and gave me a good excuse not to go to work and not to tell anyone. It was my parents I didn't want to know. They suffered enough by my living in America.

The two weren't caught but in that hot court room, surrounded by sweaty, nervous people, I shivered.

Time heals but there are constant reminders. Thanks to the media, rape is always in your face. You can pick your TV show or movie for how you want your rape served tonight. I was naïve thirty years ago, but I am cynical today. Still, my half hour of horror is far outshone by the subsequent hundreds of thousands of hours of cherished life, love and laughter. Ike, however, could still gleefully strangle my two rapists, as one had tried to throttle me.

I am good at masking my little issues, and Dan didn't notice anything amiss.

"I expect they think you're my Mom," he said.

Oh, how wrong they would be, I thought to myself.

"Did I tell you?" he asked. "I think I forgot. My parents are coming up this weekend and want to meet you. They are so pleased that you are interested in my writing. I don't know what to do. They mustn't know about any of this." He sounded desperate.

What a time to tell me.

"Well, all I can say is, I don't lie, period. And I won't lie for you. Before this I would have been glad to meet them but now, I'm wary."

His name was called. Dan had already told the prosecutor that the lawyer we met would be representing him. "Not guilty," Dan said looking straight at the judge, almost preppy-looking in his khaki pants, white shirt and Ike's tie.

When asked if he was under the influence of drugs at this moment he said, "No Sir."

The prosecutor agreed that he need not be jailed. Dan waived his right to an immediate trial. The first cycle of justice was over in three minutes. Like all the others, we tried to suppress our joy as we walked out the courtroom door and passed the metal detector. Outside we said in unison, "Phew! Let's get something to eat."

The public defender had the same idea. We found ourselves sitting next to him in a small café near the courthouse. The place was full – always, a good sign. Dan took a quick look at the menu and prices, checked his wallet, and said, "My treat."

Money was going to be a big problem. With Dan not wanting to tell his parents about his arrest, he had talked to his brother about helping him out. His lawyer told us his typical fees for such a case, not cheap. We talked about it as we ate our grilled cheese sandwiches with extra pickles.

"I wonder if I should put myself in his hands," Dan said, nodding toward the adjacent table.

The man's bowl of chili and can of iced tea was sandwiched between piles of official files. His gray hair flopped over his high, lined forehead, and his glasses lay on top of one of the piles. His shoulders seemed to sag beneath the weight of public justice. The poor man, I thought. We should give him a break and let him eat his food in peace.

Nevertheless, we took advantage of his proximity and Dan summarized his situation. "Look," he said indicating the case files. "These are some of the ones for tomorrow that I need to review when I get back to the office. We have more than we can handle. We do as good a job as we can for everyone but it's not the same as having your own defense lawyer. Presuming you are telling the truth about no previous arrests, you will probably be able to plea bargain. But my advice, son, is to tell your parents. You need their help if they are willing and able."

"Sorry, I just can't do that. But thanks for listening."

The defender and I exchanged looks and sighed.

* * *

"I'm going to beat this," Dan murmured on the return journey.

"Remember," I said, for the first of many times, "you can have the best lawyer and they can have the lousiest case but you show up with dirty urine and you can wave freedom goodbye."

It was then I noticed the sores on his arm again. "What's with those marks? They look painful."

Dan looked at me with a sideways glance I'd learned to recognize as a warning. "I sat on the beach last night, smoking a cigarette, by myself. And I jabbed it into my skin and held it there as long as I could. I do it when I feel so filled with guilt that only by hurting my body can I balance the mental pain."

I cringed.

Then Dan rolled up the legs of his pants, above where his shorts normally reached and pointed to more islands of ugliness on his thighs, in various stages of healing.

"That's not normal, Dan, hurting yourself like that. It worries me."

He shrugged, pulled the pant legs back down, laid his head back against the headrest and closed his eyes.

Oh shit, I thought, realizing the vulgarism was becoming common parlance when I talked to myself.

On the way back, I stopped at the art supply shop to pick up matting board. Dan came in with me. When he saw it would take me a few minutes, his anxiety got the better of him and he asked to borrow my cell phone. A moment later he was blurting into it: "Damn, don't you understand, you can't back down..." He could be heard across the room.

The shop assistant, a young woman about Dan's age who had served me numerous times, glanced at him and then at me. "Is he your son? He's real good looking."

"No, just a friend," I said to her and to him, I hissed, "For Christ's sake, be quiet. Give me my phone." We left without my supplies.

"What in the hell is going on?" My nerves were stretched.

"I'm sorry. I didn't mean to embarrass you. My brother was thinking of pulling out from helping me with the costs of all this. He's back on track though."

It was late afternoon when we drove into the parking lot of his grandmother's condo. Before going home, I needed to reconfirm, "So you are serious about staying clean?" He said that he was.

"I seem to be always thanking you. I don't know how I would have managed today without you." His words were heartfelt, and for the present, truthful. I drove away satisfied the day had gone as well as it could. It had been a long day, as much interesting as stressful. I had to admit, I felt useful and challenged.

One thing weighed on my mind, those islands of ugliness. I remembered the term used for such behaviors from my days as a nursing supervisor, self-mutilation.

Many of those patients hadn't been admitted for drug addiction. They had even more complex psychological problems.

* * *

After the bike, the day in court, and learning of Dan's cigarette burns, I was exhausted. I hoped Ike would soften. I wanted to be able to cuddle up next to him, and hear him say, "It'll be all right, keep doing your best, I'm behind you."

I missed the feel of his body. I missed my head on his chest listening to the steady rhythm of his sixty-eight heartbeats per minute. Lubb-dupp, lubb-dupp. Instead he made a snide comment about "that surrogate son of yours."

He stayed rooted on the couch by the TV. I went to my computer friend. Silence was prudent and cuddling was for the birds. But I couldn't help saying, "He's NOT my son" with staccato precision as I marched away.

I needed to talk to someone, so I tried Greg's number.

"The guy's a loser. Drop him. I don't want him in the house."

* * *

The next morning, I called Dan and reminded him that we were going out of town for a few days to celebrate our anniversary and would return with Lauren, our granddaughter. "Don't forget, my parents will be here on Sunday," he, in turn, reminded me. Great, the day after we'd get back.

As Ike and I drove towards D.C., we passed a group of orange-clad men picking up trash from the side of the road under the gaze of their prison guards. "That could be Dan some day," I commented

"Serve him right."

81

7

An Amateur Intervenes

It was Lauren's first visit with us without her parents. She settled in fast and when Ike and I were busy she was content to watch her new Elmo video. Dan came over to show me his writing and let me know the job was his, but he hadn't gotten a start date yet. He was quick to mention that this was his tenth clean day.

Without thinking I asked him to stay for dinner, then, remembering his previous babysitting experience, asked him to watch Lauren. I told him the two of them could shuck the corn. It was fun to watch them. Dan really seemed to have a way with kids and Lauren certainly relished his attention.

Ike's furrowed forehead spoke volumes. Once again I forgot to ask him before inviting someone, let alone Dan, to dinner. It was a sore point. Ike complained that I would ask the world around for a cup of coffee, spot of tea, or even supper at a whim. I didn't see the problem; I always cooked and washed the dishes when I invited people home. "But you never used to ask people around like this," Ike would bemoan.

"By the way," I said, "I should have mentioned this but Dan's parents might pop around later. It seems they want to meet us."

"I have nothing to say to them. What if they ask about their son? Am I supposed to say he rescued two people from a burning house and spent last weekend in the hospital?"

Ike asked. "And where's my bike? I saw a different one in the garage before I went to bed the other night and then it was gone. He sold it. I know, and why hasn't he told me?"

Dan and Lauren finished the corn. He had made her think she was helping while he did all the work. They sat down together and pretty soon she was getting him to draw cartoon characters with her crayons.

* * *

The phone rang.

"Oh, hello," said a male voice, "is our son, Dan with you?"

"Well, yes," I replied. "We are just about to have supper. Dan has told us a lot about you and we are looking forward to meeting you. Why don't you and your wife join us for dessert?"

I turned around. Ike wore his if-looks-could-kill expression.

After I hung up I said to Ike and Dan, "We'll keep them so busy talking, showing them around, they won't have time to ask us anything. I hope they like the key lime pie I'm defrosting."

"Mom'll love it but Dad won't have any. He never eats dessert. You won't believe it but he's never had a drink of alcohol in his life. Not one."

"Oh, he'll eat dessert," I retorted. "That's what I invited them for. I'm sure he'll have a sliver."

There was a knock at the door. It was another of my writing colleagues, a friend of both Ike's and mine. I wanted him to see some of Dan's writing and thought he could help validate the quality of it.

Ike said, "Welcome to the mad house. You want to stay for supper? Christina's already invited perfect strangers."

I went to introduce Dan to our new arrival. I found Lauren with her crayons and Dan on the other side of the room, using our phone.

"Yes, they're coming here, on their way, now," I heard him say before he saw me. Dan was pacing, speaking in urgent cryptic phrases, his eyes cast down at the floor. "You've got to get me the money", I heard him say and guessed he was talking to his brother. Dan's mind was miles from Lauren or writing.

"Get off the phone, dammit," I hissed. "Now."

All I recall of dinner was small talk. That covered all our anxieties. We were still finishing our steak when Dan's parents arrived. It was like greeting other guests at a cocktail party, our age, predictably well-mannered, wishing to be somewhere else.

Our writer friend left, giving me a wink of good luck, and how the heck did you get into this? I kept Dan's parents busy, showing them around and reading them my poems. There was little opportunity for probing conversation.

"May I offer you some coffee and key lime pie?" I asked.

"Just coffee, black, thank you."

Dan gave me a raised eyebrow and a grin. This was a man who sat bolt upright, listened attentively, and spoke judiciously. Dan's Mom accepted her slice graciously. She sank into the couch next to him, her hand occasionally stroking his knee. Dan put his arm around her shoulder and she let her head rest on his chest. She filled conversational gaps with pleasantries about the weather and cooking.

They mentioned how great it was that Dan had met us. They asked about Ike's mental health background, and were delighted that I thought Dan had some writing talent.

It was just starting to get tense when Lauren announced, "Potty, I need potty, I need Granny to help me." What a little love! By the time I was finished helping her, she was ready for bed, and our visitors were ready to leave.

I heard Ike usher them to the front door and then Dan said, "Look at this. It's a medal Christina's Dad was given by the Queen." He was referring to one of my prized possessions, the C.B.E. that my Dad had been awarded after he retired. Under the framed medal and certificate signed by Queen Elizabeth and Prince Phillip was a photo of my parents and me, dressed to the nines, at Buckingham Palace.

* * *

As I tucked Lauren into bed, my mind wandered back to that phone early one Saturday morning in June, 1981. It wasn't a normal time for my parents to call, but what was really strange was that each of them was on the line, one in the bedroom and the other in the kitchen.

"We've got some news. We've known a couple of weeks. We couldn't wait to tell you." Mum said.

"How do you feel about coming to Buckingham Palace?" Dad asked.

"What are you both talking about?" I had no idea.

"I got a letter from Number Ten a couple of weeks ago, asking me if I would be agreeable to the Prime Minister submitting my name to The Queen for her approval that I be appointed a C.B.E."

"Dad, that's fantastic. Congratulations. Now, remind me: the C.B.E.?" I had never been a royalist and couldn't remember which of the awards that were announced in the newspaper in conjunction with the Queen's official birthday was which.

"Commander of the British Empire, one down from being a knight, K.B.E. It was in The Times this morning. Other than your Mum, I couldn't tell anyone until the news was official. I can take two family members with me. It's a good job there is just you and your Mum."

Four months later I was there. My dilemma had been what to wear. How often does one get invited to the Palace, after all? My two good friends, Anne and Leslie, had grown weary of listening to me telling of my hopeless excursions to one mall after another. They were real shoppers. After a day with them I had a navy blue, slim-line wool suit, a fuscia blouse, winter cream large-rimmed hat, and navy shoes. We still laugh about it. Mum had to lend me the gloves.

I remember how nervous Dad was as we waited at our hotel for the ride to the Palace. Dressed in black tie, tails and top hat, he was practicing his approach to the Queen, looking down at the instructions he had written on a scrap of paper:

- walk forward with back straight
- bow in front of her
- address her as "Your Majesty" but only if she says something first
- bend forward so she can place medal around neck
- bow again and walk backward four steps
- turn right to return to seat

Mum and I would have laughed but we were too busy checking each other's outfit and adjusting our hats.

I remember how pleased Dad was when the Senior U.S. Liaison officer offered his chauffeur-driven car. It showed the esteem in which Dad was held by his American colleagues. In fact, just the previous year, the National Security Agency had presented him with a bronze medal "in appreciation for your many personal contributions to our common endeavors."

My most vivid memory is the radiant look of pride on Mum's face when the Queen put the medal around his neck. What a long way they had both come, together.

* * *

"You won't find many of these in Bethany," Ike said easily enough but made no effort to extend the visit with more of an explanation. Bungy started to yap and they left with vague promises of seeing us again later in their stay.

"That's the last time Dan's putting a foot inside this house," Ike mandated. "I don't like him. I don't trust him. He sold my bike and hasn't said anything about its being missing. He lied to me on the phone – he told me he went away and he didn't. I retired from social work and I'm not taking on a new case. He isn't my family and I don't think he's good for you. You can do what you want. That's your business. But I'm not having any more to do with it."

"He didn't sell your bike. He certainly was careless and let it get stolen but he didn't sell it," I protested.

Ike's response was something between an elephant's hmmmmph and an orangutan's splutter. He went upstairs and read Lauren a long story. She was asleep in her crib next to our bed within a minute of our goodnight kiss.

* * *

I awoke very early and immediately slid out of bed. Ike's breathing continued undisturbed, resonant and rhythmic. Lauren's was remarkably similar, thanks to enlarged tonsils. It sounded as though a couple of hours of solitude would be mine. I think best in the quiet of pre-dawn, before I take the meds that both ease my limbs and loosen the structure that keeps my thoughts in check. My conscience and I needed to have a serious debate.

This was my logic: first and foremost, Ike had said I could do what I want. Yes, I had promised Kim that I'd work in partnership with him. I recognized continuing to see Dan could be construed as missing the spirit of my agreement with her, but I convinced myself I was within its letter. Thus the question was whether helping Dan was sufficiently important to warrant continued negativism at home, and the potential of disruption to treasured family relationships.

I fleetingly gave thought to whether my own needs might be part of the problem. Could it be possible that my desire to be useful was clouding my perspective? He was a user of drugs. Was I a user of his situation? Did any of this make any difference?

My early morning analysis continued. I could no longer consider Dan as an entity unto himself. By introducing us to his parents he had opened the door to his being part of a larger unit. Dan's parents clearly respected and trusted Ike and me. They were close to our age, shared some of the same interests, and could have become friends under other circumstances.

No, I decided, I couldn't be a friend, helper, whatever, of Dan's and live a lie to his parents. Dan would have to tell his parents everything that was going on. If he did that, I'd see what role, if any, there was for me.

By 5:30 AM, my plan was made. As soon as Lauren woke up, we'd get dressed, make our breakfast and have a little picnic on the beach she loves so much. We'd return by 8:30 and I'd call Dan and tell him that we must talk. The early hour would alert his parents that there was an issue. We'd go from there. Then I'd tell Ike my plan and ask him to watch Lauren until I could get things from the previous day sorted out. He would sigh and acquiesce with a frown.

This would be quite a day, I thought as I swallowed the first seven of my daily pills. These little round prescribed wonders had better not let me down. I was lucky to have a chemical imbalance that was socially acceptable, with dopamine fixes covered by insurance, but that couldn't avert my uneasy tummy that morning.

* * *

It became the most difficult morning of my life. Never have I felt so much responsibility for another's future, perhaps being. How can that be after the issues in my own family's rollercoaster of living? The difference was the unknown. I had entered the lives of strangers to play a role for which I had no training or experience. I only had instinct.

We were on the top floor of a high condo with a wall of glass windows opening to a narrow balcony. The sun shone warm and bright outside. The condo was cold. The room was like a goldfish bowl with no escape. Outside the vast Atlantic beckoned like an invitation to jump in and drown one's troubles.

I applied my Dad's often-repeated advice, "Think before you speak." I held my breath each time Dan or his Dad stepped onto the balcony, alone or together. They never touched. Dan's father's mask of normalcy was close to cracking.

Reluctantly, but voluntarily, Dan told his parents that he was still using drugs, that his recent stay in the second treatment program had, in fact, been a disastrous failure. "I had my first joint within half an hour of leaving the place," he admitted.

There was silence. It was as much as he wanted to confess, and more than they wanted to hear.

"I have known Dan for just three weeks, and you since yesterday." I spoke haltingly. "Let me ask you parent-to-parent: if there were more news, more bad news, would you be able to deal with it now? Dan is very concerned that you have reached the end in what you can handle."

The silence was deafening. I alternated eye contact with all three. Each looked at me but not at the other. Dan's eyes bespoke dread, like a deer caught in the open. "Please don't make me tell them," his eyes screamed piercing my heart.

His father's eyes riveted on me, like a hunter facing his own gun.

Dan's Mom's eyes traveled the room, looking for escape. "Would you like a cup of coffee?" she said, fingering the cushion that lay on her lap.

I was worried she would get me off track, interfere with my concentration. I continued without responding: "I just want to validate that if there were more news, you would prefer to hear it now not later. You'd prefer to hear it from Dan, not someone else."

"Dan?" His father turned to look at his son. Dan's shoulders crumpled, he wilted back in the chair, and sighed away his balloon of feigned bravado.

Out came the whole sordid matter about the arrest, going to court, possible consequences. He spoke quickly, quietly, succinctly. All three were brave and composed, acting out learned behaviors from their upper middle class family ethic. This is what I had counted on, that they would behave properly, suck it up, postpone emotion for private times, do as Ike and I would have done.

Over and over again, Dan's father repeated, "You'll never know how much time I spent with him. Every free moment. No father could have given his son more time. Baseball, we had a camp every summer in our back yard. Going to ball games, I adjusted my work schedule around him. No father could have given his son more time."

They couldn't see why I was still willing to work with him, especially when they discovered Ike's attitude.

"That's really bad news," said Dan's Dad. "We like Ike and were pleased that Dan would have someone with his experience to talk to. Can I do anything? Would he change his mind if I asked him? What about you? This puts you in a difficult position. Oh my God."

Dan couldn't believe it. He wasn't used to someone following through with something unpleasant. "You mean I can't see Ike any more. We can't go fishing? Because I hadn't told him where I really was that weekend? Because of his bike? It wasn't even a fancy bike. I really like him."

Dan's comment about the bike bothered me. He just doesn't get it, I thought to myself. Where is his remorse?

"You've lost Ike's bike, too? How much was it, Christina? I'll pay for it," said Dan's Dad.

I mumbled something and moved on. It came up several times more but I said, "No thanks." I'd lent the bike to someone for whom I knew I was taking a risk. It was a symbol of trust that spoke the truth far more than words – my choice, my responsibility. The bike remains a symbol.

The last thing we talked about was therapy. Dan's parents refused to help him financially. That included no lodging expenses after they left his grandmother's condo. They had been counseled not to enable him. He must work and support himself. They couldn't answer when I asked them where he was expected to stay. He had no money and, once he was working, he wouldn't be paid for at least a week. "He either comes home with us or he's on his own two feet."

I insisted that if I were to remain involved, he must have professional counseling in addition to going to one of the twelve-step programs. I wanted to hear the objective view of a reputable counselor. I wanted to know whether I was a hindrance or help. Dan had told me his parents would never pay. He was wrong that time. They agreed to fund the counseling. I would pay, provide them with receipts, and they would reimburse me.

* * *

When I got home, I considered the matter of conscience again. I felt it was morally right to continue supporting Dan. I had led him into the confessional, he bared as much soul as he could reach, and committed to staying clean. I could not walk out. I didn't think I would save him, I just believed that the timing of our meeting, the coincidence of our writing, the intensity of the last three weeks, and his lack of other reasonable options precluded my giving up on him.

"It's your business, not mine." Ike was resolute. "I'm taking Lauren to the park. And when are you ever going to get some rest? You are retired and you do have Parkinson's, if you've forgotten."

I couldn't answer that. I hadn't slept more than a few hours each night for weeks and never took naps. I went to my silent friend whose presence focused my mind and soothed my soul. I started writing. By the end of the day, I finished a piece for Dan's parents and inserted the one photo of him I had taken into the Word document. I was pleased I was able to remember how to do that and felt mentally strong again. But as I lay down in bed, I realized how rigid my legs and arms felt. I grasped my left hand with my right and bent my wrist back and forth. There was a definite bump, bump, bump in the middle of the movement. I tested my elbow and felt the same cogwheel action. It's one of the ways I tell how effective my meds are.

When I returned the next morning to Dan's parents' condo they greeted me stoically. I was reminded that they had been through this before. My summer sojourn was their perpetual winter.

We talked about Dan's writing – what had drawn us together in the first place. His father said he'd never read anything Dan had written. I told them that this was the vehicle through which I hoped I might be able to make a difference. I gave them the piece I had written earlier to help them understand:

> *Writing may be his salvation, the spark to be kindled...he is good...he communicates with his reader and reaches their core...his images are vivid, his metaphors have real meaning... his real self, the Dan you know, shines through...and yes, it's quirky, not easy reading but it has character, distinctiveness... a stream of consciousness awaiting his crafting...I don't know if I can help him rekindle his own spark, just a little bit. But I promise to do my best.*

His father shook my hand and thanked me again. "If he could just have the last four years back," he said.

"He needs to go back to age five," I told him. Though insensitive, it was the truth but I knew I must be tired to have blurted it out.

Dan went downstairs to my car with me. "You were right. They needed to know. It's like a weight off my shoulders. Thanks yet again!" His little grin appeared for the first time that day.

"No big deal. I'm glad you're still talking to me. I thought I lost you at one point yesterday when I was pushing you to 'fess up. And just wait until tomorrow. We've got to agree on some rules you know, a formal understanding between us. Oh gosh, and find somewhere to stay."

"Yeah, I know. But I should find out tomorrow about when I start work. Just waiting tables and serving at the counter but at least it'll be the start of making money to pay off the lawyer. I'm hoping to live off tips. If only I had been able to get a real job earlier, I wouldn't be in this awful mess."

I went home. Ike kept his back turned as he peeled potatoes for supper. When you are exploding, and need to tell the events of a critical day, irritation becomes rage. How dare he bully me with self-righteousness? He's not perfect himself, dammit. His trying to play the "I know what is best for you card" just wouldn't work.

Hell, I thought, I've taken risks for people all my life. Why should I stop now? Just because Dad told him, in a moment of vulnerability, to take care of me? I'm not that bloody disabled yet. I got myself a bowl of cereal and stalked upstairs. I didn't need his lousy supper or his pious silent treatment.

Kim called later in the day. She wasn't her usual chatty self. For the first time, both our kids had sided with one of us, and it wasn't me. "How are you managing with Lauren?"

"Just fine, thanks." But I knew Ike was shouldering the responsibility. We would be taking her half way home to meet Greg the next day. That will make it easier to help Dan, I thought with just a twinge of guilt.

* * *

Two days later Dan and I sat in the car in the parking lot outside the condo. His parents had left. He was about to be homeless. It would make the contract I was about to give him even more difficult to live up to. "Here are the guidelines," I said euphemistically.

The very need for this document changed our relationship. The rich and famous may be writing pre-nuptial contracts these days but I wasn't aware of any friendships with written rules. It was a document I had taken care writing. I'd never written such a thing before but I knew what to include. To be sure I hadn't left anything out, and to reinforce the importance of keeping Ike informed, I asked him to review it.

"It looks alright," Ike said after reading the first draft.

"You've got the rules well documented but what about the consequences. What are you going to do when he fucks up? And he will."

I went back upstairs and worked on it some more. I wanted Dan to know that the contract was going to be difficult for me as well as him. I wanted him to see the risk I was taking. I wrote each bulleted item precisely. There was no "out" clause. I knew it and didn't know what to do about it. That was the part Ike had needed to see.

Dan spent time and care reviewing each line.

- "This one is going to be tough. I know it's what I have to do. I'm so stupid to get arrested."

- "Yes, I will be honest with you; you know me too well and have done so much."

- "Okay, absolutely no drugs. But this bit about not being around any active user, I don't know. It's everywhere you know, that'll be difficult."

- "Yes, counseling might be good, but twelve step, I've tried it before, it's not for me. But okay, it's on your list."

- "So if I screw up, you are out of the picture, unless I get myself into treatment and then we could be writing buddies again?"

Line by line we went through the list until he came to the bottom bullet.

- "One last chance to continue my risk." He looked at me, leaned over and touched my hand.

"It's really difficult for you at home, isn't it? You don't think I can get Ike to change his mind about me? Are you sure you don't want to get out?"

I didn't tell him that I thought the likelihood of his being able to stay clean was minute. I wondered whether his lack of remorse was the clouded conscience of an active addict, or whether it went further back. I still felt staying involved would help him more than hurt.

He could choose to take advantage of this offer, or not. His destiny was in his own hands. We both signed and dated our copy. He folded his up and put it in his wallet.

"This contract is binding and I am human," he said. "I'm just being honest."

8

Who's the User?

I arranged for Dan to stay in the loft of the exotic plants shop. My friend had already met Dan and I told him the entire situation.

"He can stay as long as he's clean. I could use some help around here anyway."

I told Dan the rules of his living arrangement as we sat on a bench at the far end of the same boardwalk where he was arrested. Our bare feet were perched on the railing. Then he told me the stark reality of cocaine addiction. Sun bathers, body surfers, and the symphonic sounds of waves were in front of us. Board walkers chatted as they strolled behind us, seagulls squawked above. There was space on either side of our bench but nobody bothered us. In our conversation, we were in a different world.

The following is my interpretation of what Dan told me of his experience. It is the essence of his words, plus my reading between the lines. He told me I got it right.

I learned of using the plastic cover of a compact disc, almost as an altar to place a sacred piece of rock, on the tabernacle of your unmade bed. Then comes ritual as part of anticipation for the main event.

You lock the door, get out the notepad and pencil for the explosion of creativity you always expect, and then you tidy the bed and clean the surrounding area so you can later detect if a speck of a crumb of the holy grail has wafted to the floor.

Ready now, for the favorite credit card to press down on the rock, but not completely, yet. You know that at the end you're going to want, no, you're going to need more. So you cut off a little bit of rock and place it in the corner of the room and bury it in the carpet, so it will be there for the finding.

Back to the credit card, you press down slowly, evenly, meticulously; the finer the powder, the more even the effect, the longer the high. The tension mounts. Using the credit card, you then break the pile of dust into two long lines, like the white streaks against a blue sky from a jet plane.

Now carefully, you ration your stash into separate piles. You are almost prepared to receive the sacrament. You roll a dollar bill into a tight tube and take a deep breath. You are so ready. You kneel against the side of the bed, place the tube into your nostril and snort.

Snort. Pigs snort. And pigs grunt and squeal. And pigs grovel in the mud. And when the last of your sacred rations is snorted, and your mind is spent, your penis shriveled, and you crave one more orgasmic thrill, one more extension away from your pain and boredom.

Then you grovel on the floor, like a pig, looking for one little speck that may be lying undiscovered. And when there is no more, you crawl on your hands and knees towards that precious spot in the corner where, planned so deviously, that little opportunity for a flight to the heavens or a glide into hell still awaits.

It is no wonder that addicts are considered as society's pariahs, like lepers, unclean of old. "Yeah, and they should have a bell hung around their neck or a scarlet "A" emblazoned on their forehead so we know who they are," someone expressed. It's hard to "get it", to understand the craving associated with this all-consuming, all-contaminating disease. A lifetime illness that has an insurance number but no matching coverage, more patients in jails than in centers of rehabilitation, and no program for early detection and prevention.

* * *

Not having a home or office where we could meet was frustrating. I wanted to be able to ask him to follow up on our contract and to keep up with his writing. The inability to get him hooked up to the internet, my primary source of information was so annoying. I wanted him to research such matters as NA meetings or bus schedules. The telephone at the shop was for business purposes only. There was no table, privacy or quiet.

Dan's job at the pizza parlor came through and kept him busy six days a week. The job provided him with a legitimate bike to get back and forth to the loft. It was the one he used to make deliveries. He took Monday evenings off to go to the writing group, and worked his schedule around counseling sessions.

He liked the work, his manager and the coworkers. "You're our favorite waiter for our whole vacation," I heard the father of a family of six tell Dan as they left a thirty percent tip. He wore his carefree facemask along with his uniform tee shirt. Both fitted him well.

The downside was that at close of business every day, the opportunities to have a drink, smoke a joint, or go to a party or a club were there. The dilemma was powerful: the lonely loft, bare except for his bed and a suitcase, or nightlife with people his age. The appeal of the beach, the rhythm of waves, the calm of a shared toke and the allure of pretty young women – it was seductive.

Counseling probably worked more for me than Dan. At the first session Dan was asked whether or not he wanted me to sit in the first two sessions. These would focus on intake rather than therapy. "Sure," he agreed nonchalantly. He knew the game. She was his fourteenth therapist. She asked him to describe his relationship to me in NA terms.

"My safety net," Dan responded.

"What about enabler?"

This time I responded. "I'm not his enabler. I'm involved to help him stay clean, not to enable his addiction."

I found the term stereotypical and belittling, but the rest of the session was enlightening. I realized for the first time the depth and breadth of Dan's problems with addiction: drugs of all types, alcohol, gambling, and danger.

Dan lived off pizza and tips from his work. Every Tuesday, he gave me his paycheck to put aside for him to pay his lawyer's fees. Occasionally, we went out to eat but I certainly didn't want to start gossip by being frequently seen out in the company of an unknown man, less than half my age, without Ike. Bethany is a small town.

The loft was working as well as possible but I felt awkward being up there with Dan. The bed was the only place to sit. Usually I arrived before Dan was up. Sometimes I felt like a mom going up the stairs to kick her son out of bed, wondering if he would ever grow up, annoyed to see yesterday's clothes sitting on the floor. Most of the time, I'd be in my mentor role, either bringing my writing or rushing in and out with the calendar to confirm who was doing what that day. I even brought him our leftovers.

But there were times during that hot sultry August when I'd climb up the stairs and hesitate before calling out my usual "Are you decent?" I may have wondered once or twice if the covers had joined the clothes on the floor, inadvertently kicked off a sleeping, naked body in the heat of the un-air-conditioned night. There were times when I sat on the side of the bed and drifted into fantasy before catching myself, stretching and pushing up and away from the suck of the air mattress. It was our eyes and minds that connected, never our bodies.

There was opportunity and temptation, but this was not a Mrs. Robinson relationship. I love Ike. Dan loved marijuana or whatever. Neither of us was stupid. Yet during those days Ike would cynically call Dan, "Your boyfriend," knowing my hackles would rise.

* * *

When we saw each other, we talked first about life without drugs and second about writing. It wasn't as much fun anymore. I missed our free flow of ideas, the thoughtful conversations of two open-minded people. Yet, still there were times when our writing buddy relationship would emerge.

Once we went kayaking. It was his first time and my fourth. The young woman who rented the boats joked that I would be the senior paddle partner this time. We started off laughing as Dan got the hang of using the one paddle, but moving in a straight course on a windy day soon kept each of us focused.

We aimed for a little island and paddled up on the beach. It was a haven. The sun was high in the sky causing dark shadows from the intricate piles of driftwood that littered the shore and overhung the bay. Only the screams and squeals of sea birds interrupted the pervasive quiet. No tree grew straight. All were stooped like old men, gnarled by the wind. It felt so comfortable together yet alone on our private island, each in his own space, never trespassing. He lay back on the beach, cap covering his eyes, deep in thought. I spent ages taking just the right photograph.

"Don't you wish this afternoon could last forever?" Dan said, stretching his shoulders, getting ready to paddle again. He must have read my mind.

* * *

Later that week, driving to our second meeting with the counselor, Dan talked of demons that kept him up at night. He kidded the counselor that she hadn't asked him for a urine specimen yet. "I'll catch you when you're not expecting it," she retorted.

I was pleased she now called me his mentor. Later I wrote: "*In his mind the fight never lets up, Never a night without temptation, Desire vs. truth, Wrong vs. right, Who's wrong? Who's right? Me or they? You or we?*"

On the return journey, he asked out of the blue, "So you really wouldn't still be my friend if I just had the occasional joint?"

His words took me by surprise and it took a minute or so before I answered. "You know I believe a real friend will stay a friend no matter what... but our circumstances are different. Friends don't have rules and, thanks to you, we have our damned contract. I really believe, friend to friend, that you mustn't do drugs any more. It's not good for you in the long run. I know you said just a joint but we both know that it will be one snort of coke next and God knows what would come after. In the short run, I don't think that prison would do you or society any good. You're not the kind to relish being some big guy's girl friend! So no, friend, our relationship would change if you started again."

"The trouble is, you want my recovery more than me." Each of us told the truth, and neither liked what each other had to say.

* * *

One of the things we still argued about was Dan's inability to get to one of the twelve steps, NA programs in the area. I maintained he was afraid to go. He responded that work was his priority. He needed to make money, not moan about drugs. He said that he would go when he had time.

My Internet search indicated an NA group had open meetings at a local church hall. Okay, I thought to myself, I'll find out what goes on at these meetings, and why Dan is so damned reticent about attending. I told Dan and Ike that I was going.

I was a bit nervous. What does one wear to look nondescript? Might I be rejected because I wasn't an addict myself? Rejection would be embarrassing in a strange kind of way. Somehow, I wanted to look as though I fit in and yet did not belong.

I checked with the group leader to make sure I could attend and he confirmed the meeting was open. It was my intention to sit unobtrusively in the back but the previous group had forgotten to leave the key to get into the church. This meant we all sat in a semi circle on the grass outside, just on the edge of where the grave stones started.

The sight of a motley gathering of about 20 people doing their best to look clandestine attracted the attention of neighbors who called the police. The officer, who I had met before, gave us permission to conduct the meeting quietly. He glanced at me quizzically. I wondered what he was thinking as he politely averted his gaze.

A young woman gave me a piece of paper that I assumed was general information. Shortly I realized I was one of a few who had been given an NA principle to read aloud. This was the kind of attention I wanted to avoid!

Reluctantly, I stammered, "Hi, I'm a friend of an addict so I'm not sure I should be reading this." Gestures indicated I should continue.

I learned a lot about addiction that evening, listening to fears shared with nonjudgmental peers. The focus of the meeting was complacency. It seemed that was as dangerous to an addict's continued recovery as turmoil. I was glad I'd gone, and knew Dan would benefit from this group.

"You really went? Alone?" Dan was incredulous. "What did you say?"

"I said I was a friend of an addict," I replied. "And they told me I could come back any time, but you need to come by yourself. They think you're full of excuses, actually they said 'shit', and you're scared to come because they'd see right through you."

"Oh my God. I don't believe you really went. For me."

"I went, I learned, I achieved my purpose."

There was nothing more to say.

He never went.

* * *

Ike remained adamant about not having anything to do with Dan and that included hearing anything about him. We only spoke of essentials.

One day when I came home from seeing Dan, Ike handed me an envelope. "State Board of Nursing," he noted. It was time to renew my license. I kept it current the whole time I worked for the consulting firm. But, now, what was the point? I tore the form into shreds, dropped them into the waste bin, and shed a few tears. Another symbol of my former identity was gone.

My friends and fellow exercisers at the pool wondered about me. I missed classes because the time coincided with my driving Dan to meetings with the counselor. And I rarely stayed afterwards to relax in the hot tub, as was the usual pattern of our little group. Most could not understand my choice of helping an addict of brief acquaintance over doing what my husband thought best for me. On the other hand, others trusted my judgment, were supportive and understood why trying to make an impact in another's life was important to me. They all cared.

It wasn't just Dan that was taking my time. After my book came out, I received a call from a town councilman asking if I would be interested in taking photographs to be used in Bethany's new website. Without hesitation, I said yes. It was an exciting opportunity.

During the six weeks of summer, I took over twenty rolls of film. I photographed local officials, city workers including the police officers who had arrested Dan and had seen me at the NA meeting, town events and scenery. Between touching base with Dan, keeping up at home, and two trips to Washington, I would rush out to take photos of lifeguard competitions or fire fighters in action.

Some events took all day. I photographed the July 4th Parade, the replacement of the town's totem pole-like structure called Chief Little Owl, and the dedication of a park to commemorate the town's centennial. At the park they buried a time capsule that included my little blue and gold covered book. To think twenty-five years hence my grandchildren might be invited to its disinterment. I would be eighty-three. No way with Parkinson's would I be there too.

Finally in September, I took part in the town's tribute to September 11th. This was especially moving for me as I was given the opportunity to read from my book as part of the program on the boardwalk. Beyond the sea of faces, the veterans' honor guard, and the firefighters' bell for their fallen comrades, churned the vast Atlantic. I felt at home.

* * *

"Don't you ever slow down?" Dan wondered. "Are you sure it's me on drugs, not you? Dopamine, amphetamines, cocaine, they're all related you know."

I thought of the irony of the question for a moment and had a smile on my face as I replied, using a couple of verses from a poem I wrote with a rap beat:

> *My brain is my being*
> *My mind my control*
> *I never used dope*
> *Never crossed my mind*
> *I like my mind the way it is*

Clear and perceptive
Alert and objective
I like my mind
The way it is

Not for me the scene
Of extra sensory
Virtual surreality
I get my high from
Watching the sky
Making the most of each minute
Until my pen runs dry
And the camera won't click
Just won't click, just won't click

* * *

On the way to the writing group at the book shop, a couple of days later, Dan seemed different, more pensive. The radio remained off.

"So what do you think happens to you after you die?" he asked.

"After you die?" I repeated in my best remembered "how to talk to psychiatric patients" way.

"Come on, remember I've been in therapy, I'm asking you to hear your answer."

"Well I believe that when you die, you are forever dead and gone. There is no life after death for you, the individual. However, the way you do live on is through others, either through your genes to the next generation or in the memories of others. To me, when I am at the point of death and am comfortable that in general I will be remembered well, it will be as though I were going to heaven. In other words if I believe I've done my best in life, I think I'll die happy."

At the writing group meeting Dan opened one of his filled binders to the back cover. He explained he had written on it after meeting a Jewish born, Christian convert at a diner where he ate breakfast. "You are one of God's chosen people," Dan said the man told him. Then he read: *Looking down these floors to the hot concrete, I fantasize my own mortality. What would the descent be like? How long would it take to fall nine floors? Years. How big would be the splat on the sidewalk?*

The group attendees, including me, didn't know how to respond.

"I'll never forget his reading that poem," the writer of children's books told me later. "Thinking about it, kept me awake that night. He seemed so nice and so troubled."

The Tuesday meeting served to reinforce the unease of the last few days. I felt he was using again, or close to it. He had managed to avoid me, and didn't look me in the eye. I felt an urgency to confront him with these changes, as well as the morbid nature of his writing. I knew that this would be my last window of opportunity until Friday. Friday was our next appointment with the counselor. It would also be Dan's birthday.

Once again, I wished we could just go straight home, have a cup of tea and just talk like normal people, but Dan was banned. I decided it would be helpful to have a third party's perspective. Maybe Billy could help.

"Dan, how about getting a bite to eat before we drive back?"

"Sure," he replied. He had found a book of Jack Kerouac's writings and was debating whether to spend his precious tip money on it. "My birthday present to me," he decided.

"Billy, we're going to get some supper, do you want to join us?" Billy looked at me as I tried to signal him with a cock-eyed wink, and knew something was up.

"Why not?" he said.

Dan sensed my invitation to him hadn't been casual. We walked in silence across the parking lot to an outdoor table at a nearby restaurant. I was never good at small talk and I'm even worse now.

We ordered crab cakes, French fries and iced tea for three before I jump started the conversation.

"Dan, you know, Billy knows a bit about what has been going on since you joined the writing group. You're starting to act weird and I'm concerned that despite what happened, you are either using again or about to jump in the deep end."

"Hey, what's going on, man?" Billy said softly. "You look like you've got a load on your mind."

Dan muttered a bit about things being okay, but then told Billy about how the court situation was getting him down, drugs were available, and America was two-faced about its attitude towards drugs.

"Give me a break," I sighed. "So what? Tonight's problem isn't America, it's you."

Billy did his best to help Dan feel comfortable, and to get me to stop interrupting. "We've all got our battles to fight, little things that too easily get the better of us and end up taking over our will."

Dan focused on swirling a fry in a mound of catsup.

"Look at me," Billy directed.

Dan hesitated before looking directly across the table. "So what do you see? What's my addiction?" There was silence. I wasn't sure what Billy was going to say. He opened his arms, encircling his plate as he exposed his girth. Billy is a big man, tall, with broad protective shoulders like the Daddy Bear in the Goldilocks story.

"Food?" Dan said at last.

"Yeah," Billy replied. "I've lost over one hundred pounds at different times but it's a struggle every day to keep from eating what I want."

I realized how lucky I was to have another true friend, a man with the decency to share painful problems to help another. Dan told Billy the facts of his arrest and the situation with the court. He described what the lawyer had said about the tough stand Delaware takes on drug crimes.

Then, like a broken record, he recited his excuses. It was an evening of truth telling and withholding. Dan was clearly at the end of being able to resist temptation. He was back to rationalization.

* * *

I got a call from the counselor.

"Remember the last time Dan came," she said, "and he spent ages in the bathroom after I asked him for a specimen? Well, he's using again."

I called Dan's Dad.

"I am at the end of what I can do to help," I told him. "Perhaps he just hasn't sunk low enough yet."

"He mustn't go to jail. He's got to stay clean. My God! If he doesn't know that now... I'll support him going to another program, just one more time," he said, adding the condition that Dan must stay there for its duration. I was relieved and absolutely agreed.

"Thank you so much. I don't know why you've done so much for Dan. We all knew it was short term, but you've given his Mom and me the break we needed."

I tried to explain that there was reciprocity to our relationship, that he filled the void of accountability I so missed from work. I didn't tell him how his son made me feel young again. He wouldn't have understood.

It was apparent that I had indeed retired at the right time. My face was tight, my stiff legs and arms ached, and I hardly slept.

"Damned Parkinson's," I thought. I wouldn't be in this situation if I were still working. This little bit of stress was starting to upset my equilibrium. I wondered if I should take some more medicines. Of course, this was just the thing that Ike expected to happen.

Damn.

It was the Labor Day weekend. I decided to throw myself into taking photos of the events that mark the end of summer. In Bethany that means a New Orleans-style funeral march on the boardwalk, complete with a jazz band and crazy costumes, and a special lifeguard celebration.

For twelve weeks or so, the men and women of the beach patrol drilled every morning, sat long hours on cold, calm days struggling to stay alert, fought rip tides and high waves on days that surfer kids call "sick", found little tykes who had wandered from careless parents, and competed against other area beach patrols.

As a team, they'd saved many lives. The rescued, of all ages, were uniformly as embarrassed by the attention from gawking strangers as grateful to have their feet on firm

sand. Most, but not all, said "thank you" before their heroes
dashed back up the beach to their perches on high.

It is the tradition that at end of the final day of the season,
the bronzed beach icons let down their guard, along with
their uniforms, in a final plunge into the surf. Needless to
say, the sensitivities of Bethany's keen-eyed board walkers
must be protected from any over zealous nudity and thus a
police officer is assigned to the sand. To my amusement it
was one of the officers Dan had recognized on the day of his
arrest.

"Christina, please don't take photos." The captain of the
lifeguards sidled up to me. I turned to the sea just in time to
see a very white, bare behind glistening atop a very tanned
pair of legs in a perfect jackknife dive over the crest of a
wave! "Don't worry!" I promised.

Dan, the police officer, and the lifeguards were all about
the same age and, generally had the same opportunities –
but such different summers.

* * *

After much fuss and deliberation, Dan agreed to go to another rehab program. His parents arranged for him to be admitted to a Scientology-based facility in the southwest. He called me many times from there and I called him even more. By that time, I needed him more than he needed me. He had people to talk to. I did not.

He needed to get away from me, his family and anything associated with his drug experience. I needed him to feel useful, to have meaning in my life with Parkinson's.

But one afternoon, he called me on my cell phone as I was on my way to Rehoboth. "Where are you?" he said.

"Going over the bridge. Getting my dose of God," I replied.

"You've got to buy a book. It's just been released. I could have written it."

"What are you talking about?"

"Kurt Cobain's journals. And the worst thing is, my book bag is gone. They sent a kid home 'cause he broke the rules and somehow my stuff went with him."

"Jeeze. Surely it'll be returned. Don't let it mess you up."

The bookshop clerk pointed to the display table of books about prominent people. I sat, engrossed, on the carpeted floor, my back against the shelves. Between the covers, the copies of pages from spiral notebooks, the hand writing, even the words were almost identical to what I had seen so often in Dan's missing book bag.

I wrote one last poem for Dan, the way I thought he was feeling, and mailed it that evening.

> *For half the day*
> *My world is in darkness*

For half of the day light
Clouds block the sun
For half of the sunny days
I stay inside

87.5% of my life
I live in the dark
A mushroom, a fungus
Nourished by dirt
And dung

But when the sun
Shines high
I am alive
Energized
I write

I write of
My fears
My hopes
My pain
My beliefs
My very life
In spiral note books
On lined pages
In pencil and pen
It pours out
The way
I think it
Abstract, symbolic
Unrefined
Awaiting crafting
Awaiting

The book bag is
Gone

It's not a death
Of a part,
It is me
My image
My reflection
My essence
I stand naked
At noon
Shadowless

Imagine a man
Struggling
To find meaning
Identity
Energy

Imagine
Having the future
Awaiting crafting
For ever
Awaiting

Cobain,
Do you hear my scream?

On a couple of occasions Dan told me he had learned that the public telephone he used was "bugged". He asked me to call on the staff phone instead. But the next time I called, an automated recording told me that the connection from my home phone number was prohibited.

The justice system required Dan to return to the Sussex County courthouse twice more. His parents drove him back and forth from the airport, keeping him in their sight as they promised his counselors. At their invitation, I sat with them in the courtroom and watched the proceedings. Dan wore a blue, smartly ironed, open neck shirt with his khaki pants this time. He didn't need Ike's tie and we didn't play HANGMAN!

On the first return visit, the lawyer thought it best to postpone proceedings. He wasn't sure their plea bargain would be accepted by the prosecution. The sticking point was the charge of resisting arrest. We stood outside the courthouse thinking that the trip had been a waste of time, money and mental energy.

Suddenly I said: "If the prosecutors are going to be in touch with the police about this before the next trial, don't you think it would be helpful for their last recollection of Dan to be a good one, rather than of the night it all happened?"

They all looked at me as I suggested, "Why don't we drive down to Bethany and see if the police chief is in so you can apologize properly?" It was something to be acted upon, not just fruitlessly talked about. "Let's go," I said.

Dan and I drove together. His parents followed. I don't remember the radio being on. This time it was Dan who couldn't deal with distraction.

I did ask him if there were any more islands of ugliness on his body. "No, now that I've been in the program a while, I haven't felt the need."

The police station in Bethany is adjacent to the town hall, opposite Chief Little Owl. Dan and I sat in the car under its ever-vigilant gaze. His parents drove up behind us. We each remained in our own vehicles.

"Do you think he'll see me?"

"Don't know until we try."

"What on earth am I going to say?" Dan's hands cradled his head. His glasses lay in his lap. His hair was now short, his Bethany tan long gone and his grin had faded into tight lips.

"Just tell the truth."

As we got out of the car, Dan's father rushed up. "What are you going to say? Should I come in too?"

Dan said nothing and walked up the ramp to the police station. He held the door for me and we walked in.

The police chief recognized my name, and agreed to see us.

"Well son...?" he asked looking Dan straight in the eye.

"Last time I was in here I came in the back door, in handcuffs," Dan started. "I'm so ashamed."

* * *

The last time I saw Dan was when he returned for his final day in court about six months later.

He pled guilty to the lesser crime of possession of marijuana. The resisting arrest charge was dismissed. He was sentenced under the first offender's program, involving addiction counseling and probation. He had already met the requirements due to the intensity of his rehab program and his agreement to stay with it.

As we left the court house, Dan gave me a final hug, and thanked me again. I don't think he saw the tear in the corner of my eye.

"Enough saying thank you," I chided. "That's what friends are for."

"You saved his life," his Dad told me, as he shook my hand before driving Dan back to the airport.

Then he added, "Maybe it's time you focused on your hubby, now."

9

Sixties People

"Hubby" is not a term I use to refer to Ike. And Ike was not who I had in mind when I announced to my parents, "I want to meet real Americans."

I was close to finishing my senior year in high school, my first year in America, and was confronting the issue of what to do next. Going to college or taking a year off to travel in Europe seemed the only acceptable options amongst my privileged classmates.

"Americans all get sick", I asserted. "I want to become a nurse." My mother couldn't understand it. She hated to be around hospitals and sick people and couldn't understand how a daughter of hers could want such a thing.

Dad tried to talk me into getting the university education that he never had. However he backed off when my SAT results came back. They were the first multiple choice tests I'd ever taken and I hadn't yet learned how to play the game.

We settled on a three-year nursing program at the Washington Hospital Center in Washington, DC for two reasons. First, a hospital-based program was more akin to English nursing training, and second, I would have just one year to be by myself after Mum and Dad went home to England.

* * *

My first day in nursing school opened my eyes to the real America I hadn't known. There were a hundred of us, all girls, on two floors of the dorm. The building was a nine-story single wing with double-occupancy rooms down each side, and a common bathroom in the middle of each floor. We were each assigned a roommate except one, our only classmate of color, Janice.

She and I chatted that evening, along with the rest of the girls as we found the hospital cafeteria, got stuck in the elevator and giggled nervously. Janice's parents moved to America from Jamaica many years before. Her father was a minister and she had always wanted to be a nurse. I knew it was wrong that she was the single one to sleep alone that night. I thought what a silly mistake it was. I didn't know enough then to be angry.

The next day the administration gave us the opportunity to swap roommates. Mine had discovered someone she already knew so I moved in with Janice. It was the start of a lifetime relationship. It also was my entrée into my third culture: English, white American and colored. Funny to say colored now but that was the term of the era, preferable to Negro and before black became beautiful.

I was blissfully unaware of prejudice as I grew up in Cheltenham. There didn't seem to be anybody to be prejudiced against. "Rule Britannia" was just a song to be sung with gusto, nothing that made me feel superior to anyone. I never learned American history in English schools and my year of the subject in high school had been dates, battles and presidents, not social conditions. I liked my roommate and her parents from the start. I grew to love them as I became part of their extended family.

It was fortunate that Janice's circle of friends and family was extensive, because there was no huge flow of social invitations from our classmates. With my own limited number of acquaintances in this country, I was happy to become included in her world of family get-togethers, clubs and parties. Janice's family and friends came from roots where it was long realized that education was the key to equality. Their lives were middle class just like all the white Americans I had met among my parents' friends. Thus to me their difference was citizenship not race.

It was during the last quarter of my first year of nursing school that I met Ike. I was assigned to a residential three month rotation to study psychiatric nursing at St. Elizabeth's Hospital. St. E's, as it is known to all who have been there, is comprised of an imposing complex of Civil War era brick buildings, surrounded by a wrought iron fence. Each entrance is guarded as much to prevent patients escaping as to deter unwarranted visitors. Every door required a key to get in and out.

St. E's has been home to such luminaries as John Hinckley, Jr. who tried to assassinate President Reagan and Ezra Pound. It is no wonder that, at seventeen, I was intimidated.

It was the custom for new student nurses to greet their patients by having a party on one of the wards. Ike is a story teller and I have heard his version of how we met on numerous occasions:

"I had just got back from lunch when my head nurse said, 'Weaver, I want you to work across the hall on Six this afternoon. There's no male over there today and the new students are giving a party.' 'No problem,' I thought to myself, 'I can check 'em out while I'm looking out for them'.

"The party was in the day room where the patients stayed. Back then the ward was filled with chronics, mainly schiz's but some manics too. We called the hospital Mother 'lizabeth because

it was the only home many of the patients knew. Some had been there more than twenty years. So I'm walking down the corridor to the day room, checking the doors along the way, making sure they're all locked. The day room's this big open space with bars on the windows, heavy orange and green plastic-covered chairs and scuffed tan colored walls. The chairs are heavy so nobody can pick one up and throw it if they get out of control.

"Just as I'm passing by, the nursing station door opens. The nursing station is like a goldfish bowl looking out on the day room. 'Staff only.' And here come two students, striped uniforms, white starched aprons, caps on their heads, looking all prim and proper...and scared too. They were carrying a full sheet cake with white frosting, one that the hospital bakery made. Back then, we had a dairy, a post office, fire department, our own farm with cows...it was just like an old town with walls around it.

"Suddenly the cardboard under the cake started to buckle. I didn't think, I just dove to the rescue and saved the cake. Kinda looked like Art Monk diving for a catch and making a touchdown. Those girls were so grateful. One was blushing. She had a real cute accent and was pretty too.

"'This party might be alright', I thought. So I played my cards real cool, played pool with a couple of the patients, sat down on one of those big orange plastic covered chairs and interacted with others as we ate the cake. Then someone turned on the record player and the students got the patients dancing. It was real nice.

"Time to make my move. 'May I have the honor of this dance. Miss Long?' I asked, looking at her badge.

"You can call me Christina and I'll call you Sir Galahad," she said.

"That was it. I was hooked from the start."

* * *

I dated Ike for about a year before I told my parents. It wasn't just his race that kept me from telling them, it was the fact he was nine years older than me, and hadn't graduated high school. Not exactly the credentials any parent hopes for. But as the time grew closer for them to return to England, I thought I had better introduce them to the guy who I now considered my boyfriend.

"Stay in your seat. I'll get the car door," Ike said as we drove up to my parents' house.

I glanced ahead. The net curtains shifted a bit. Yes, they were watching. By the time we got to the front door, it had opened.

"Mum and Dad, this is Ike. I expect you guessed."

Everyone was on their best behavior. Dad did what made him the most comfortable, offering Ike a beer. Ike was glad to accept. We ended up in the basement chatting and playing ping-pong for an hour. It was more like an audition than an inquisition. Ike was surprised by the civility of his welcome. He hadn't realized my Dad was a diplomat and my Mum had welcomed more strangers to parties in her house than most people had family gatherings.

They asked him about the civil rights movement and listened carefully as Ike told them of his experience on the Mall in Washington the previous year. "Seeing Martin Luther King and hearing his Dream speech was amazing", he said, "But what was really inspiring was the size of the crowd, how many white people came to it, and how positive we all were."

My parents were dismayed at the thought of leaving me in America for a year with Ike as my boyfriend. (In fact, he was my first and last). They wanted nothing more than my long-term happiness and success but they would never be rude.

"I like them," Ike said as we got into the car again. "I don't know who was most nervous. Thank goodness your mother smokes and your Dad drinks beer."

Later, when pressed, Dad commented. "It's his age that is the worst part. He is a man. I'm not going to be able to gently convince him to stop seeing you."

* * *

One day Ike took me to meet his parents in the rat-infested neighborhood that was their home. The front door was unlocked.

"Mom, Dad," Ike yelled. "It's me. I've brought someone to meet you."

There were noises in the bedroom. Ike tried to open the dark green, paint-chipped door but it was locked. A funeral home calendar praising the Lord, and a fly swatter from the same establishment hung from a nail in its center.

Eventually we heard the key turn. Ike looked at me and turned the knob. His mother was crawling back under the covers of the bed. An empty wine bottle sat amidst the clutter of the bedside table. A man's pants were crumpled on the floor and the toilet in the adjacent bathroom flushed. She didn't know where her husband was. We left without my saying a word.

"Well at least you know what you're getting into," Ike said as he kissed my cheek and smiled.

I looked past the camouflage into his sad, gentle, brown eyes. Sons raised by alcoholic mothers learn to expect disappointment.

It was an inauspicious start to a relationship in which I still call Ike's mother, Mrs. Weaver.

* * *

When we graduated in June 1966, Janice's parents gave me a book of poetry inscribed, "With fond and loving thoughts. We shall always cherish the memory of your friendship and hope that you enjoy happiness and satisfaction in your chosen profession." The book still sits on my bedside table.

* * *

I returned to England for a year after graduation from nursing school. I thought I loved Ike but I wanted a final year in England before making the hard decision to leave all else that I loved to return and get married. I hoped to practice nursing in England but found that one must be twenty-one to get licensed and I was still only nineteen.

What was I going to do? I wondered. I was already thinking about the money I would need for my return trip. I went to London. Oxford Street is known for its shops and for employment agencies. I got off the tube at Marble Arch station and tried the first agency I saw. A mini-skirted young woman asked me to complete the obligatory questionnaire. She was looking through it when the phone rang.

"Would you like to be a nanny?" she called across the room.

"Sure," I said without confidence.

I called Mum on my way to the interview. "Who is Douglas Fairbanks, Jr.?" I asked. "I may become the nanny for his grandchildren."

And that is how I spent my twenty first year: almost one of the family, in an upstairs/downstairs world. Most of the time we stayed in the manor house just north of London where Mr. Fairbanks's daughter and her family lived. They could not have been nicer or made me feel more at home. One of the perks of my 24/6 job was to have a cup of tea in bed each morning, where I was joined by my two little charges. They were sweet and mischievous.

From the five-year old I first heard the word "fuck" spoken aloud. A woman driver cut in front of our car and in his high-pitched, upper-class, English accent I heard him yell: "Go fuck a duck!"

During my ten-month stint we joined the Fairbanks several times in their posh row house around the corner from Harrods. I met the rich and famous, movie stars and royalty, as well as the people who served them. My favorite recollection is of Mr. Fairbanks coming downstairs punctually at nine o'clock each morning in his silk dressing gown, a fresh rose perfectly positioned on its lapel. He was ready for breakfast.

Once a week Fred the gardener would come in the big kitchen waving a familiar blue airmail letter-form. "Another one from your young man, it must be Wednesday. You've got him hooked alright."

I'd read Ike's letters for the first time between ringing through the heavy wash of nappies (English for diapers), and hanging them on the line to dry. During that year I received forty-eight letters. It was what convinced me that Ike was right for me.

Ike carried a little notebook with him wherever he went and jotted down all of the little things that transpired he thought would interest or amuse me. One letter noted *"I guess you read in the newspapers that we can now live in any state in the union due to the Supreme Court decision on mixed marriages. Things are getting better slowly."*

It was 1967. The letters served the purpose of a journal that neither of us would have thought of writing at the time. I still have all the letters. As my twenty-first birthday loomed, I started to make plans to return to America.

My parents were now confronted with the realization that their beloved daughter was leaving them to live in America with a man of color and with few resources. I was frustrated. I would tell them excitedly of my plans, seeking their advice, and they would give no response at all. I decided to write to them to explain my feelings.

Eventually my Dad sent me a response. I still have it stored in the same box as the letters from Ike. It makes me cry to read it now:

My Dear Christina,

I am so sorry to have taken so long to reply to your "problem" letter but I wanted to be able to think quietly at the weekend & not to write when tired.

First I must explain why we have been avoiding the "problem" in discussions and letters. The best analogy I can think of is a person who knows he must have his right arm removed: now under those circumstances as in ours, one would be foolish to do other than try to forget it & think, talk & write about more pleasant subjects.

You may feel I am exaggerating in using that analogy but our unhappiness is twofold. First, we are worried about your future marrying a colored man at the present stage of American history and secondly there is the unhappiness which would be there were you marrying a white American.

Every parent hopes that he will be allowed to follow his daughter's married life from not too near but equally not too far. I will not dwell on this but I think that you know what the feeling of this hope means in our particular case.

Thus our avoidance of the subject is due to an increasing sense of unhappiness and not to any feeling of coldness or hostility toward you. You have made your decision & we would certainly not be so petty as to refuse advice (spelled with a "c"!) if you need it.

The only thing you cannot ask of us is that we be happy at your decision or even neutral. This is just more than the human nature is capable of. Your offer of money to help us attend the wedding was touching but it would be too harrowing an experience & I am sure that on reflection you would not wish to inflict it upon us.

We do not intend to go away in July just before you depart & must all do our best to prevent an emotional outburst which will do none of us any good. This will be more difficult than I can say in words & the only remedy is that which I have been applying i.e. that of an ostrich who buries his head in the sand & pretends the trouble does not exist. I wish that there were a more rational way but we are all at heart more sentimental than rational in family matters.

I hope that you will now understand our feelings as clearly as you have shown your feelings to us. As you say, it is not the end of the world, but for us it must be a very sad time & I fear that there is nothing any of us can do to prevent it,

Your loving Dad

Later Dad told me I could always come back, no questions asked. How different was the reaction of my parents to that experienced by others I knew. Several friends from the sixties who ventured into interracial marriages have yet to be reconciled with the families from whom they became estranged.

* * *

After a year back in England, and three days after my twenty-first birthday, I boarded the Queen Mary, bastion of Britishness for the hurly-burly of New York's docks. A telegram was on my pillow when I arrived at my cabin. It was from Mum.

"Good Luck," it said. I cried all night, knowing the risk I was taking would hurt her the most. I never told her how much that telegram meant to me.

My all was contained in two steamer trunks and a wallet with ten dollars. What will I do if he's not here? I wondered as I descended the gangplank. Get back on the ship, I told myself. This time, strains from Procul Harum's *Whiter Shade of Pale* filled the air. Their manager at the time was Mr. Fairbanks' son-in-law's brother. How do longshoremen know exactly the right music to play for debarking passengers?

Never have I been so pleased that Ike's face was black. It stood out amongst the sea of waving white arms and beaming faces. He was there. He always would be. He was my rock.

Three weeks later, we were married. We were sixties people, filled with the belief that Martin Luther King's ideals would become our reality.

10

My Rock

Ike and I were married on a Friday afternoon. We honeymooned for the weekend, including cruising on a paddleboat built for two in front of the Jefferson Memorial. I started work on the following Monday.

Not only did the Washington Hospital Center train me as a teenage student nurse, it continued to teach me for the next seventeen years. My children were born at the Hospital Center and now Kim is growing up in nursing there, too. Many of her colleagues used to be mine.

Recently she said to me, "Mum, I talked to a nurse today who told me she worked evenings with you. She wants to know if you remember that night during the riots when you both went up on the roof."

That night was the start of a period I'll never forget. My colleagues and I watched the smoke and flames as Fourteenth Street was set ablaze. There must have been about twenty of us including staff, doctors, security and patients.

One patient pushed his own IV pole. He was wearing his hospital gown, robe and paper slippers. As we looked out over the flames in the night he said quietly, "That's where my house is."

I remember the black faces of patients and staff who lived in the neighborhood. They huddled together in the background. The doctors, interns and residents, most of whom had only a temporary attachment to the city stood to the fore. "This is history," one of them said.

It was 1968 and Martin Luther King had just been assassinated. Eerie was my word for it. Behind us was the darkness of a cool April evening. Ahead were the fires. Then, like a firework show, there were red, white and blue flashes of emergency vehicles and, eventually, National Guard trucks. The noise of sirens accented the stench of a city on fire.

Ike had called my nursing unit. "Stay there until I can pick you up," he said. "You'll never get a taxi home tonight."

Once he got there he waited an hour for me to finish my shift report. I was lucky to have a relief nurse at all. Since Ike had arrived, National Guard soldiers had taken their stations on the street-corners, enforcing a curfew. On the five-mile journey home we were stopped three times by soldiers with rifles aimed at us. Each time, we were ordered out of the car, questioned about what we were doing, and our car was searched. It was an America few Americans have experienced. We went to bed exhausted.

Worries about Mum and Dad nettled my sleep. They would hear the news of the riots and worry about their daughter living in the midst of it. All that Ike and I believed in seemed to be on the line. We lay for a long time in each other's arms before slipping into love, giving into the flow of our own bodies and blocking out the ugliness around us.

The next morning we awoke to the sounds of male voices, indistinct but clearly angry. We peered through the blinds. Across the street hundreds marched, their hands holding baseball bats, their faces anonymous under ski masks.

Later there were knocks on the door. "You want some cheap booze? Or baby food? Or shoes?"

"Man," Ike told one, "get away from here. You've put us back to before Rosa – given up our self-respect for stolen goods from our own neighborhoods. You make me sick."

* * *

Those early years were not easy. It was our pride as much as our love that kept us from betraying doubts, fears, and even regrets. Ike brought a pattern of established bachelor habits to our marriage. I hadn't noticed these when I was in nursing school and somehow they'd remained unmentioned in his weekly letters.

"What do you mean you're going out? Do you have to spend every bloody Friday night with the boys playing poker?"

I couldn't believe it. We had just purchased my first car, a secondhand VW bug, but I still didn't have my license. Ike was teaching me to drive, but on this occasion he had taken the wheel for the trip to the grocery store. We were returning with a paycheck of groceries.

I had planned to celebrate the car and paycheck by cooking a fancy dinner. But no, stupid me, it was Friday. With both his arms embracing brown paper bags, I looked at him marching toward the apartment. I wanted to smack him but instead yelled, "Forget it, I'm leaving."

Then it struck me. I have no money, can't drive and have nowhere to go. For the first time, I wished my Mum lived around the corner. I remember thinking, "I made my bed, damn it, and it's mine to lie in."

My bed in fact was Ike's double bed. And, as double beds are made to be shared, so compromise necessarily carried the day. Ike bought the double bed set when he got out of the army. It is dark wood and has two bedside tables and two dressers. He picked the one he liked the best, even though it was expensive and bought it on a lay-away plan. Double beds seem to have become single beds over the years as Queens and Kings have taken over as the norm.

Ike bought a bed to last his lifetime. In the drawer of the headboard he had put a hunting knife with a leather sheath. "For protection," he explained. Whenever we moved, and the bed was taken down, the knife was sharpened and put back in its place.

Ike would have his darned Friday nights, but once a month we would have our own little ritual, dinner at a different restaurant. We broke our rule at the El Bodegon, a Spanish place where the maitre d' came around to each wrought iron table pouring sangria down customers' open mouths. It was far too good to go just once.

Now we both laugh as we recall that neither poker nor cozy dinners survived the advent of kids. As Ike puts it, there was our BK (before kids) and AK (after kids) time.

* * *

Ike is a person without artificiality. In his sixth grade autograph book, one of his few childhood possessions, a girl wrote:

> *When you get married*
> *And live upstairs*
> *Don't fall down*
> *Putting on airs*

Ike stayed true to the verse. I suppose his friendly "what you see is what you get" personality is what attracted me to him. It's also why so many people like Ike from the time they meet him.

He is a storyteller. With our numerous acquaintances and friends he has enjoyed a continuing audience over the years. Those who listen often hear about a different America than the one they have known. "We really enjoyed sitting by the fire and listening to Ike's war stories," is a typical notation in our guest book.

These are true stories I have heard so often, I almost feel as though I was there. I expect every family has one like Ike, who evokes the raised eyebrow, and the "Oh no, not this one again!" He usually starts with tales of his "coming up" in Barnes, middle of the boonies, South Carolina.

"I was so little they put me in a shoe box filled with cotton. It acted as an incubator. That's what sharecroppers did. Yes, I was country before country was cool. They looked at me in that shoe box and said to my Mom, 'he's so cute – just like a little monkey'. So everyone started calling me 'Monk'. I guess that's how most nicknames start.

"How did I get my name, Ike? Well, when we came to Washington, I was teased on the playground. I'd say 'let's chunk some ball' and they'd laugh at me and say I must have just fell off the turnip truck! Then they heard my brothers call me 'Monk' and they'd jump and hop around calling my name and laughing.

"Well, one day, I was walking close to Pennsylvania Avenue and I saw a crowd of people gathering on the sidewalk, cheering. I ran up to see what was going on. It was Eisenhower in an open top limo, wearing his uniform and waving. Everyone was yelling, 'I like Ike'. And I said to myself, 'that's it, from now on I'm Ike'. I went home and told everyone my new name and that was the only one I answered to. Been Ike ever since.

"There was no work for coloreds back then. My parents left my next two brothers and me with my grandparents while they went to Washington. Mom wasn't even twenty then and she found work at a dry cleaners. Dad started on the railroad. It was Grandma and Granddaddy who raised me. They were strict, no nonsense, churchgoers. Yes, Baptist that's what we all were back there. I remember standing next to my grandmother at The Lone Pine Baptist Church singing the 'Sweet chariot coming for to carry me home' spiritual. Everyone could hear her voice, she sang it so loud.

"My Granddaddy used to tend the cemetery. I remember him going off with his garden tools on a Saturday and coming back with the Reverend. My Grandma would shoo us outside and we'd have to wait for the Reverend to finish eating before we were allowed back in. 'Hush your mouth or you'll feel your Granddaddy's belt', Grandma would say if we complained. If it was summer though, there was always something to eat like peaches, plums, raspberries, watermelon and walnuts. We just helped ourselves."

* * *

It takes no more than a rainy day for Ike to regale visitors with his storm story. *"One day, my uncle came to visit. He had just come back from World War II and brought me and my brothers some candy. Anyway there was a terrible storm, lots of thunder and lightening. I was scared, so to cure me my uncle put me outside and closed the door. It was so dark between the lightning bolts. Of course, there was no electricity, no glow from distant cities.*

"I got wet and cold but the longer I was out there the braver I got. I stood by the little patch of garden my grandfather gave us boys. We grew everything in it that he grew in his, and in the fall we dug up the white potatoes and sweets and wrapped them up and put them in the earth mound for use all winter, just like

he did. *I looked at the tomatoes I had strung up on spindly poles and I figured if they could still stand tall in a storm this bad, so could I.*

"*When the storm was over, the door was opened. 'Ya scared any more boy?' 'No sir', I told him and I never was. My brothers had been watching for me out the window. When we were all tucked in the one bed in the little back room, we munched our candy and I boasted that it weren't no big thing.*"

These South Carolina stories are his favorites because they are memories of simpler times: two strong grandparents as role models, a clear set of values, consistency and love. "I wish you could have met my grandmother." Ike has told me many times. "You would have loved her."

* * *

Life changed drastically for Ike and his brothers when he was around ten years old. His parents had two more boys since coming to Washington and they wanted their first sons with them in the city.

"*I remember my Grandma saying when we got to the train station, 'Now Monk, you're in charge of your brothers. I talked to the conductor and you can tell him if you need anything. Here is a box of food. Don't start eating until 6 o'clock because it will take all night to get there and you'll be hungry if you eat too quick. Look after your brothers for me, and look out for your parents too'.*

"*Well, I may have been in charge but we hadn't been on that train half an hour when we opened the box. Grandma's fried chicken smelled so good. And a big biscuit for each of us, a piece of my favorite lemon frosting cake as well. We didn't have anything left to eat from the South Carolina border to Washington, D C. Mom and Daddy were at the station but I*

thought we'd come to the wrong place. I saw trees. I didn't think
there were trees in cities. It was the best part of getting there."

There is a gap in Ike's stories until he gets into the army.
He doesn't like to talk about the difficulties his parents had
encountered. From happy kid in the country, Ike's life fast-
forwarded to big city boy burdened by the responsibility of
being eldest.

Ike's demons include his parents' gradual retreat into
the miseries of alcoholism and their regular moves from
one lowly set of rooms to another. He went to work at age
twelve, to make money for the family and as a way to
avoid being home in the evening.

Few have heard Ike's stories about how his prized
collection of comic books disappeared. It happened when
he came home from school one afternoon and found his
family had been evicted. While his parents tried to find
somewhere to stay that night, their meager possessions
had sat on the curb where passersby could pick through
them.

On another occasion, after Ike realized that most
families had a set of plates and bowls to eat from, he saved
up his money from working in a local deli to buy them a
real set of dishes, fresh out-of-the-box new. He had felt so
proud that Christmas when his Mom used his dishes to
serve a festive dinner. Pride turned to bitter
disappointment when within a year they had all been
broken or chipped. "They threw them at each other when
they were drunk," he told me.

The best part of those years was his job at the deli. He
used to get on the trolley bus every day after school and
travel down Washington's Georgia Avenue in Northwest
to Southwest. It was a corner deli, owned by a Jewish

family. There, Ike found the respect, discipline and love he had known from his grandparents.

He swept the floors, stocked the shelves, helped the customers with their grocery bags and, best of all, he was in charge of the penny candy counter. *"Pop didn't like serving all the kids when they came in. He was old and didn't like bending down to where the candy was so the kids could see it. Of course he knew I ate some of the candy but that was Okay.*

"I was like family. They wanted to adopt me and take me to Baltimore when they retired. They talked about sending me to college, but I stayed home. My brothers needed me."

He dropped out of school in the tenth grade and started to work full time.

* * *

Sitting around with a group of friends, solving the world's problems, I hear Ike saying, *"It's not taxes that are the problem, it's how we use the money. Worst mistake this country made was to get rid of the draft. Okay, some people got around it and went to college or whatever but for most young men it was a great equalizer. It gave them a chance to get out of the confines of their growing up, go places, meet people, and open their eyes to new possibilities. If we'd kept the draft, we wouldn't have all these young boys in jail."*

When encouraged, Ike continues his story telling. *"I volunteered for the army early, figured it was a good time as Korea was over and they were offering the buddy program. You've never heard of it? Well the deal was, if you signed up with two other people, you could stay together, be assigned the same unit. Shoot! We went down on the bus from Washington to Fort Jackson, South Carolina.*

"Three days after we were processed in, my friends' names were called out amongst others to go to tank training in Texas

and then they were to go off to Germany. After roll call, I went and protested to the sergeant. He laughed and said, 'Private, welcome to the United States Army.'

"*After basic training, I went home for fifteen days before getting on my first plane – to Lorton, Oklahoma. There were some New York boys on the plane and we all got talking. They were going to stay in a hotel for their final night before we had to report to Fort Sill and they asked me to join them. 'I don't have no fancy hotel money', I told them but they said not to worry as they were getting a suite, and I wouldn't have to pay anything.*

"*We all took a taxi to the hotel. I knew we were going to have trouble when my bags got left at the curb. Yeah, the red caps were black but they had jobs with uniforms, I don't blame them. One of them looked at me, 'cause he knew the whole thing was wrong, he winked and carried my stuff through another door and next thing I knew it was with the other luggage. The leader of the group said they wanted a suite with four beds and adjoining rooms. 'Well, three of you can stay but not him,' drawled the hotel manager looking at me long and hard.*

"'*Don't bother me none,' I told them, 'I'll do like I was going to.' Those New York boys started to get ready to fight, they were so mad. I just got my bags, hailed the next cab and told the driver to take me to a colored hotel. Never saw them again. Fort Sill was so big. I just stayed alone in my room until the next morning. My friends told me later I'd have felt less foreign in Germany than Oklahoma.*

"*How did I feel? Disgusted, that's how I felt, plain disgusted. It was my first real experience with overt racism. Yes, I know that sounds strange, but growing up in South Carolina and Washington segregation was so entrenched it was all we knew. There were families who were fair complexioned, we called them 'yellow', who passed for white. So they sat downstairs in the uptown movie houses; we sat in the balcony. But I didn't feel that personally, it was just the way it was.*

"Another time Daddy got injured while he was working right close to the old Garfield Hospital. They wouldn't take him in there. He had to go all the way back a couple of miles to Freedman's, the hospital for coloreds. You have to understand this was in the mid-fifties, just before the civil rights movement took hold. Other than Mom and Pop at the deli, I never was around white people to feel the effects of racism directed personally at me before."

Ike was chagrined to discover that many of the soldiers he met knew more about the nation's capital than he did. They had come on school field trips and had seen the tourist attractions that hadn't been part of Ike's Washington experience. So he vowed to get to know his city better when he got home. That was a vow Ike lives to this day.

Whenever he reads about a new memorial that has been erected or an opening of a major new exhibit, he goes to it. All our friends and family say he is the best tour guide they've ever met. Not just because he knows the city so well but because he also takes them to the side of town where the people are poor but the anecdotes are rich.

"What in the world have I done, I wondered as I heard the loud speaker blare, 'Specialist Weaver, report to the General's office in full dress uniform at 0900.'

"It was an Oklahoma-cold Saturday in December and I had hoped to be able to sleep in. When I got there, I found I had been chosen as one of the honor guard to raise the flag at the entrance to the base for the official photograph for the 1958 Christmas card. They gave me special white bootlaces, and a white belt, and a silver cap for the occasion. It seemed to take forever to unlace mine and lace them up again!

"*My platoon commander had recommended me. He patted me on the shoulder, and told the General about when I drove him around during maneuvers and about the communications work I did using our company radio. I felt proud. He sent each of us who were there that day our own personal copy of the photograph and the card. I still have them, of course.*

"*Computers were just opening up when I got out of the army. I thought with my communications training and experience, I would have a chance. They gave us all a test to help us with career decisions after we got into the civilian world. Funny how all the white guys I knew, who I had got ahead of, were given the chance to get into government computer training programs. But then, I suppose, most of them had finished high school.*

"So I went back to the department store I'd worked at before enlisting. Trouble was, I had learned to work too well in the Army. I just did my job the best I could and one day I was told I could work in the kitchen or be fired. The supervisor told me later that my work made the old-timers look bad and I was a danger to morale. I rejected the kitchen job and went on unemployment instead."

Unemployment and Ike didn't agree. His drive and self-pride couldn't keep him down long. He heard of a job opening at St. Elizabeth's and applied to become a nursing assistant. It was three years later when Ike became my Sir Galahad.

* * *

Ike spent his entire career at St. Elizabeth's. He took night school classes on the GI bill, getting his high school diploma at age thirty-two. He was vice president of his senior class in high school the year after we were married. Six years later, he received his degree in sociology. I believe he was the first in his family to attend college let alone finish with a degree. When he retired after thirty-nine years of government service, as a psychiatric social worker, guests at his retirement party included the chief of the hospital, several physicians he had worked with over the years and numerous patients as well as colleagues.

In our marriage, Ike has always been the practical one whose favorite place to be on a Sunday morning was the hardware store. Our yard was always the envy of the neighborhood. It's a fact that Ike knew more neighbors than I did because so many of them stopped to chat with him and marvel at the height of our rhododendron bushes and the girth of his tomatoes.

As our kids were growing up and I was busy with my career, Ike kept the home fires burning. We lived in the Washington suburbs and Ike and our children were always in the minority. One day, Ike heard me describe our family as "mixed up".

"We may be mixed but we're certainly not mixed up," he rebuked me.

Not only did Ike cook supper most evenings for our kids but frequently half of their friends as well. At different times, Ike was assistant den "mother" for Greg's cub-scout troupe and I helped Greg on his early morning paper route. Ike drove Kim and her friends to school each morning, while I was her track team and swim team cheer leader. When Greg and Kim's friends needed a neutral adult's ear, Ike listened. He pushed both Greg and Kim to use their initiative and to work hard.

"We can afford to have some help around the house now," I suggested a couple of times.

"If we made the mess, we should clean it up," he would say.

* * *

Over the years Ike and my Dad had become staunch friends – an odd couple bonded by the love of me and a quirky sense of humor. My Dad jotted down some thoughts for me to include at Ike's retirement celebration:

> *Kindness to his father-in-law of an order far above the call of duty – this includes moral support during his mother-in-law's long illness and practical support to keep the family home in England in good shape, decorating,*

> *repairing and gardening, all done willingly and cheerfully.*
>
> *Ike is gregarious and loves to laugh and joke; this extends to his friendly approach to the many elderly people he meets during visits to England. He is comparatively imperturbable and takes the ups and downs of life very much in his stride. One can guess that this quality has kept him going during his long career at St. E.'s.*

Ike looked forward to retirement. Working with poor, mentally ill people was draining and it had become increasingly depressing to him that the monies that had been available in the years of Kennedy and Johnson had bottomed out with Reagan.

After I started traveling so much with my job, Ike used to joke that he looked after crazy folk all week and me on the weekend. He hoped for a retirement of peace and quiet, fishing, gardening and plenty of TV.

11

Off My Rocker

Ike knew that Parkinson's was changing me from before I retired. When he and Dad had the talk about my needing to be taken care of, they had already seen the signs. I began to think of Ike as an old fuddy duddy who wanted to hold me back from making the very most of the last few years that I had to enjoy. I resented him. And my kids too, when they sided with their father. Ike thought Dan was the beginning of the end.

"You've gone off your rocker," he told me one night after catching me surreptitiously trying to call Dan.

"You just can't stand that Dan has given a new meaning to my life," I rejoined. "You don't know how awful it is not to be working. You don't know what it's like not to be able to read or watch TV. You don't know what its like to sleep only three hours a night and have nothing to do but spend time with my computer. My computer understands me better than you do."

Indeed when Dan went into rehab, my computer and I became inseparable. Helping Dan had provided me a counter weight to balance my life. And I tried to recapture that balance by writing about my experience with Dan. It took me three months to complete the 500 page manuscript of *The Third Wheel*, which started:

> *Written for all who may wish to remember me*
> *As I am today, my birthday,*
> *July 17, 2003*

Dedicated
To my family, with gratitude
For their understanding, care and love
Of a changing me

A lot of it was about Dan, but by including stories about my parents and their lives as well as my growing up and work experiences, *The Third Wheel* also served as a family memoir. I told people that part of my reason for writing it was so that my grandchildren would know me through my own words. I even reserved time at a professional recording studio where I sat in a sound proofed room with ear phones, a microphone and a sound engineer. Reading the whole book took six CDs. I wanted my grandkids to know my voice as well as my words. So sure was I that Parkinson's would soon deny me the ability to fluently communicate.

"Yes, I've read it," said Greg.

"Well what do you think?"

I had given him the most recent draft of the book. We were on the phone, both next to our computers. "I still don't like him and have no interest in ever knowing him but I guess he gave you something to think about. After all, you always got energy from working with the younger consultants at your work."

"By the way, you got a word wrong," he added. "You shouldn't have said 'reticent' on pages 182 and 286. Reluctant is the word you should have used."

"Are you sure?"

We each looked it up. He was right. Dad would have chalked one up for Greg, with a knowing wink, if he had been around.

"If it wasn't for this damned Parkinson's, I'd never have written this book, you know," I said.

"Yeah. You know I never was able to read that book about Parkinson's you gave me. I didn't want to associate it with you. I guess I'd better get over my denial."

* * *

I may have been writing about balance but my life was starting to become even more off kilter. Literally from 5:00 am until around one the following morning, my stiff fingers poked clumsily across the keys of my computer, either writing or doing research on eBay. Research was my euphemism for gambling.

I became fixated with buying things. First, it was antique Chinese celadon that enamored me. I purchased the sweetest little frog with its tongue sticking out. I believe and hope it is over one thousand years old. I know I spent a dollar for every year of its existence!

When I ran out of places to put my celadon collection, I switched to being obsessed with the work of Käthe Kollwitz. She was a wonderful German artist of the late nineteenth/ early twentieth century who used charcoal and etching to portray the darkest scenes of humanity. As well as pictures, originals and prints, I bought books about her, and then postage stamps, coins and postcards with her likeness.

Next my attention was drawn to very old, some even slave-made, black, rag dolls. I ended up with close to one hundred, as well as a doll house that was made as a replica of the last functioning slave house in Virginia.

Needless to say, I would make it my business to be at the post office early in the morning to pick up my latest treasure before Ike was even out of bed. It was amazing what I could hide around the house, in open view, that he never noticed.

147

But I couldn't hide such things as the three huge crates with picture frames that I bought for a song. I remember the postmaster giving Ike a pitying look as we struggled to get them, one trip at a time, in the trunk of our car.

And then there was my biggest eBay win of all – an early twentieth century display cabinet and writing desk from a Manhattan estate. It is seven foot tall and decorated with chinoiserie ornamentation. I have to say everybody has questioned the number of my purchases but nobody has faulted my taste!

It wasn't so much the purchase that I wanted; in fact I gave many things away before I ever got them home from the post office. It was the thrill of placing that last winning bet, just in time to beat out my competitors.

If I wasn't buying stuff on Ebay, I was giving money away. There seemed to be so many needy people. On one occasion I was delighted to kill two birds with one stone, so to speak. From one who'd just lost his job, I bought a car. To another whose old jalopy had finally died, I gave the car. The one paid his rent, the other got to work. That gift I told Ike about.

On another occasion, I bought hundreds of dollars of old furniture and other "stuff" from a junk shop dealer who was having a hard time paying his rent. It was too much for me to transport in my car so they delivered it in a truck. I told Ike I thought he needed a hobby and he could re-finish and sell it all. Ike said I was his hobby and he didn't have time for anything else!

We aren't by any means wealthy but had been good savers while we worked. From the first time I heard the expression 401K, I liked the idea of employer matches and made sure I maxed out my contribution each month. It was to be money for our old age but I was past thinking of anything but the here and now.

* * *

During my couple of hours of sleep at night I found I was experiencing vivid dreams. In fact, I never remember dreaming much at all before. I awoke from many of my pre dawn excursions out of breath from being chased in buildings with long corridors and dead ends.

But one night, three years after Dad died, I saw him.

"He was here," I said pulling urgently on Ike's shoulder, as I sat bolt upright in bed, instantly awake.

"He was wearing his old cap and gloves and raincoat like he always did. I said to him, 'You can't be here, you're dead,' but he didn't say anything back. Then he glided around the living room, looking at the pictures and everything, and he nodded his approval. And I went to hug him, and he just disappeared, evaporated. He was so real."

Sobbing, rocking back and forth, knees touching chin, I repeated over and again, "He was so real."

Ike murmured sympathetically. He turned over and went back to sleep, but I got up and went directly to my silent friend. I read through the files of poems I had written after Dad's death. I looked at his photo on my desk, his face fading as I embraced his space. Going to the drawer where I keep my prized possessions, I took out his old cap and gloves and clutched them to my chest as though trying to fill the chasm. I needed to keep his face alive, to see the intelligence in his eyes, the concern in his smile, the sensitivity of his chiseled face. Playing with the keyboard, I recreated his face with another photo and computer graphics. I got him just right; his essence captured in a 3D glow.

Wouldn't that be the epitome of irony? My mind meandered through the remainder of the night. My Dad's father had been a spiritualist. Indeed when he died at the ripe old age of ninety two, his obituary called him the "Grandfather of London's Spiritualism". My Dad helped him conjure the atmosphere for séances in the front room of their home, when he was a small child. It was what had turned him away from religion.

Maybe Dad's old man was right when he communicated with the departed and brought hope into the hearts of his poor, predominantly female customers (and shillings into his pocket). Could that have been Dad's visiting spirit? Had he returned to tell me something? Or had the chemicals of grief finally gelled in my brain, allowing a silent wound to heal, oozing no more.

I couldn't get Dad's visit out of my mind. "You have to write about it," my best friend said after hearing my anguish. "Write it now while it's still fresh in your mind and your emotion is still palpable."

Easy enough, I thought. It can't take long to write about an event that was so short and which I remembered so precisely. But I was wrong. It's one thing to recount the facts of an event but another to provide meaning. If I were a person of faith, I would have been reassured that my Dad had gone to a better place. I would perhaps have been comforted that God sent his spirit back to me to bring his death to closure. But I am agnostic and agnostics, after all, never accept anything easily.

Now, I rationalize that it was a vivid intense dream, a chemical spark from a smoldering ember that allowed me to grieve his death, not his dying. I believe the dream was internally triggered, based on the accumulation of my experiences and the pharmaceutical environment of my brain that night.

In my system of believing, it is the memories of those who have touched me that live forever, not in heaven, but in my subconscious – ready sources of wisdom and warning, caution and comfort. I call them my angels without wings. They are my debate team for those issues that keep me awake at night and cha-cha in my gut all day!

Are my angels just another name for God? I don't think so. I don't pray to them. I just listen. They are not all knowing, they are just people, living and dead that I have known, loved and respected, people I would like to have a cup of tea with. My angels are part of my conscience. When I die they will die with me unless someone else chooses to keep them or me alive in their own arsenal of rightness.

* * *

Shortly after Dan left, I discovered the joy of Open Mic nights. I loved the camaraderie between musicians and joined a group known as the Players Club. One night as I was driving home from the Nassau Valley winery where the Players jammed, I recalled a conversation with one of the guys and realized with a grin that yes, I have new "guys" in my life now. They wear jeans and T-shirts, instead of suits and white shirts, and display their tattoos and plug in their electronic equipment with the same studied nonchalance that my other guys selected their ties and poked their blackberries. Mostly they are musicians and writers. A mixed bunch made up of all persuasions and ages, these guys are individuals connected by a passion for music and words.

Like the guys I once worked with, some have done their time on the road. They carry their guitar case or the like with the same care as my work "guys" carried their laptop bags. They've put in years traveling the circuits, playing gigs. Some have played beside people whose names I recognize, but always in the shadow. They are the journeymen of music whose sound has connected with the good-timers and the hard-timers in neighborhood watering holes across the land.

Many play just for the love it. Their livelihood comes from their daytime jobs as chefs, techies, electricians, lawyers, teachers and preachers, but when the sun goes down their saxophones wail, guitars moan, drums reverberate, vocal chords quiver, and they inhale the applause of the crowd. Applause is the symbol of love, acceptance and even adulation that is the aphrodisiac of performers.

Then there are the young ones, of whom many are good but will forever remain dreamers, "wannabes" in a business where really good is not enough. Gradually they disappear from the scene as their daytime jobs take over their dreams. But one day they return for the love of it.

Lastly are the very few who exude the talent and charisma that it takes to get to the next level. They just need the opportunity, a bit of luck and timing. They are filled with the joy and despair that only the truly passionate ever feel. And they give each gig their best; their music flows from their soul. Yet most will remain on the edge, a new generation of almost-stars.

These guys, like the work guys, are fun to be with. They share quick wit, friendly barbs and insider information. They are open to other people who have creative spirits and who appreciate their music. And they give back whatever they take in the form of encouragement, recognition and experience. And from them I've learned a new lingo. Who would have ever thought I'd be published, extolling the talent of a young, new Blues band, dropping phrases like "sound dynamics...simple, tight, roots music...rock overtones...reminiscent of Hendrix?"

There is innuendo and teasing, but the rules are still there if you choose to play by them. And they never talk about cooking, shopping and kids' carpools. And when the rest of the guys aren't around, and it's just me, my mind and my ear, their camouflage occasionally fades along with the jest, and they talk about their fears, hopes and reality. And I feel useful again.

Yes, I like the company of guys.

Somehow I lived over fifty years without music being part of my life. Soon music, or rather musicians, young people and artsy types, became my new raison d'être I began going out to different bars and coffee shops as much as five evenings a week. I was liked by my new group of friends and my poetry was too. Every week, I produced about four new poems to read. But no longer was I writing the Hallmarky-type verses like Kindred Souls that had first attracted Dan.

Now I wrote about addiction, politics, war, religion, death and insanity. To show the change in my writing, one of my most requested poems was from a collection I called, *Poems with Pith and Punch:*

Paranoia of Solitude

An empty space
Stark walls
One chair
No sound
A mirror
To look at one's own
Face
And be seen by them

153

Christina Weaver

Noise of silence
Voices
Throttling
My scream
That bug creeping
Up the wall is my
Friend
Or enemy

A full room
Chattering ants
Competing
With cacophony
A drill
To bore one's own
Eye
Deafening my invisibility

Nothingness
Routine
Almost safe
The key turns
A cocoon
Cringes
In the corner
My mind, my home

Noise or naked
Hidden or exposed
There is a fly crawling
On my wall
And spiders
Eat ants,
Caught in the
Web of my space

154

I read it to my psychiatrist on one of my regular every three months trips north to the medical center. In fact reading my poems or even full chapters from *The Third Wheel* took most of my hour's time.

I told them about my concern that my eBay habit might be getting a bit out of control. It was noted in my record and never followed up. Occasionally, the doctor suggested that Ike accompany me next time, but I didn't see the point. They never insisted and Ike never asked to join me. I thought my visits were a waste of time but I like being back in the hospital milieu that for so many years had been my living.

Every so often, the doctor of the moment would add a different anti-depressant to my Parkinson's cocktail.

"How can I be depressed?" I asked several times. "I get too much done and am having too much fun to be depressed." But they smiled at me for they knew better.

On the way home, Ike would stop at the closest Wawa to the hospital. Wawa's are Delaware's version of the 7-Eleven convenience stores. I would treat myself to a pint of rum raison ice cream.

Rum raison ice cream, by the pint, had become "my addiction". I gained thirty pounds. "Why should I care," I'd say. "Who's ever seen a fat Parkie patient? I'll be skinny again soon."

As well as writing poems, I started to write articles and take photos for local newspapers and magazines. The band, *lower case blues*, caught my fancy. They had so much potential and it occurred to me that if I wrote articles about musicians, it would help publicize them. Within a year, over fifty of my articles had been published and my photos were on the websites of many musicians.

After two years with the Players, my efforts were rewarded on the stage of the Rusty Rudder, a well known watering hole and music venue. The event was the Local Grammies and I was pronounced winner of the Poet category by Regina, the group's heart and soul, and my good friend. I bought a fancy long flowing purple and orange outfit with two long crinkly scarves for the occasion. It matched my glasses perfectly! It was a real high to be called back on stage with the rest of the winners. I was old enough of be the mother of any of them!

The Saturday after the Grammies I arranged an event for lower case blues at a restaurant in Bethany. It was a sit down dinner and concert and I had managed to get every seat sold.

Apparently, the meal was wonderful and *lower case blues* won everyone's hearts. I say apparently because honestly I don't remember the evening. Ike tells me I was too busy saying hello to this and that person and checking this and that detail to sit down for even five minutes.

We got home around midnight and by Monday my mind was still whizzing and I had yet to sleep. At last it occurred even to me that something was amiss. I called Dr. Leo at the medical center and told him what was going on.

"It's like being on an express train and not having time to get off at the stations," I explained.

"I'm the attending on call this month," he said, "I think you need to be admitted for a week or so to get your medication regime sorted out."

"Well Parkinson's is a neuro disease," I said. "Can't I be admitted in the regular part of the hospital, not on Psych?"

"No," he replied. "Changing your meds may cause psychiatric consequences. You'd be safer on Psych where we can watch you more closely. We're full at the moment but I expect some discharges by Thursday."

Good Lord, I thought to myself. Ike and I had often kidded people that we had met at St. E's – but there, we had both had keys.

What in the world has happened to me?

* * *

"Greetings," I emailed the editor of the local paper, "I'm doing my article for next week, I've got the photos taken and the interview scheduled but you'd better not count on me for a few weeks after. My Parkinson's medicines are messed up and I need a sabbatical."

"Fine," he replied, "let me know when you're ready to write again. Good luck"

By the time I got off the phone, I was already cross with myself for misusing the word "sabbatical". Of all people, me, the one who preaches about openness and honesty; the one who speaks her mind about the diminishing right of free speech in poems at Open Mic nights. Sabbatical was as bad as the word anonymous. How can alcoholics and addicts really be "in recovery" if they have to keep their illness a secret? Doesn't secrecy make an illness with a clear genetic component worse by adding the element of shame? How could I succumb to society's prejudice about mental illness by avoiding mentioning that I would be on a Psych unit?

"Sabbatical" is one of those code words used by Human Resources people for when the firm executive has had a bit of a break down and is being sheltered in an exclusive, distant but nevertheless, mental hospital. And I was using the word in the same clandestine way. No, I decided, it is better to be thought crazy by others than be a hypocrite in my own mind!

I called the editor on the phone and explained my sabbatical was actually a forced vacation on a locked ward.

"I have an idea," I said. "If I wrote articles about the before during and after of my hospitalizations, would you publish them?"

"Are you sure?"

"Absolutely, it would provide me the opportunity to find some meaning in this mess."

"Yes", I wrote in the first article before packing my bag, "I'm checking in to a psychiatric unit. Probably one of the most sane, wellness-focused things I can do. And I'm sharing it with you because it is important to me that little chemical loose screws that cause one person's blood pressure or blood sugar to rise or hands to shake should be considered no differently than those who hear voices, or become disorganized or even become addicted to

drugs. Recognizing one has a problem and getting help is what is important."

I ended the article by saying, *"I am a little scared. Not so much as to how a free spirit like me will cope with being on a locked unit but as to the uncertainty about changing my medicine regime. The trick is to determine the best combination of drugs that keeps me mobile, retains my creativity and love to have fun, while adding a bit more structure to my current haywire existence. Going to the hospital is my decision, my choice and my risk. Just as is sharing my story. For I have nothing to hide."*

12

Open Mic on Psych

"What year is it Mrs. Weaver?"

When you arrive they ask you what you want to be called. I said Mrs. Weaver, not Christina. Most people go by their first name, but somehow I didn't want to be that familiar with the staff.

"2004," I replied.

"Repeat after me: nickel, stool, pony."

"Okay. It costs a nickel to ride the pony from the guy on the stool."

The nurse smiled and completed the routine of questions. They are the same questions asked three times a day, every day, every patient. Season, location, president and what were those three words?

"Nickel to ride the pony....guy on the stool."

"Good job," she encourages. I hate that term, good job. That's what my kids tell our grandchildren when they get themselves dressed, go to the potty, or color in the lines. Good job. It works for children. It demeans me.

But I smiled back because it's their game, their rules, their keys to the locked doors. And if you want privileges and you want to land on Home, you play their game, their way.

* * *

"Smoke time."

They're ready, about a dozen patients, the ones who don't yet have privileges to leave the floor alone. Usually two thirds are addicts and the others are the chronically schitzy. You can tell them apart.

The addicts are interactive and expressive, the schitzies mutter to themselves and stand or pace alone. But as soon as the attendant opens the door to go outside they are one, smokers unified in purpose.

That leaves behind an assorted crew of folk with dementia, acute psychoses, and resistive addicts for whom not participating in "smoke time" is a punitive measure. The demented are older. You can tell from the families that visit and from their few lucid minutes that they once were regular, middle class people, the kind of people we all have as friends and relatives. People we all dread that their fate will become our own.

The psychotics are in their own world and have fewer visitors. The families that may have loved them either have problems of their own or have been through the misery too many times to make this any different. Hospitalization time is their respite. They don't need to visit. Their duty will return.

The addicts are assigned to the Red team, the schitzies to the Green team and the poor souls to the Blue team. I was on the Blue team.

The day after my admission, the doctors started to adjust and balance my doses of Tasmar and Mirapex. Three days later the balance bottomed out. My mind was in tune but for two brief scary hours, my body wouldn't work.

I had been allowed in the grounds outside and started to realize that my walk was slowing down. I walked so slowly, that people not only passed me by but also turned around to stare. So slowly, I didn't think I'd ever make it to the elevator and then to find the nurse and whisper, "my medicine, I need my medicine, please." So slow, that when I finally climbed into my bed, I stiffened into a contracted pretzel.

For the first time, I was given a dose of regular or fast-acting Sinemet. After a couple of minutes, I looked up and, thankfully my limbs began to move easier. I decided to try to walk off the rest of the stiffness and walked back and forth along the pale, aqua green corridor. But there remained insufficient dopamine for the brain to convey its movement message to my limbs.

In mid step, I froze. I'd heard of Parkinson's patients freezing before but never experienced the phenomenon myself.

"Walk," I told myself but I couldn't. I was stuck in place.

I heard another patient call for help. Dr. Leo had just arrived on the unit to see me. He rushed down the corridor.

"Lift up your leg and try to step over something," he instructed. It was a mental trick that worked.

"I'm going to leave an order for you to have some more of the plain Sinemet whenever you need it," he told me.

* * *

The next day was my deadline for the local newspaper. I wasn't allowed to use the computer on the unit so I hand wrote my piece. It took me much longer to write than usual because I had to print the words so I could read it. I planned to use the fax machine that I noticed inside the glassed enclosed nurses station.

"Sorry, the fax machine is just for medical purposes," I was told. "No, the rules can't be broken."

So I made a collect call to the newspaper. The receptionist had been getting ready to leave for the day. "Don't worry, Christina, I'll transcribe it for you over the phone," she said.

"It's long," I warned.

When I finished reading it aloud she said, "WOWey!"

It had been an indigestible day. Like eating cereal without having quite enough milk to wash down the fiber. I wasn't going to allow a few hours of difficult reality upset the flavor of the day I would remember.

I joined a nurse sitting outside my room. She was on suicide watch, my neighbor's, not mine although that is another story. He is a very big young man with a sweet smile, searching eyes and purple calves that foretold years of future peripheral vascular disease – just too much weight for ankles to bear. He was talking about being afraid of the other patients. I introduced myself, shook his hand and caught his eye for a brief second.

Two elderly patients sat to either side of the nurse, each with minds active and eyes intent but speechless. Language, the essence of human communication was gone. Together we made a group of five: One whose role was to be therapeutic and who was an expert; three patients, all of whom belonged; and me, who wasn't sure.

And now I was faced with a weekend when my doctors would be off, there would be very little to do and I was getting used to what would be my lowest dose of medicine that would keep me mobile. The following week, we were to try varying doses of supplemental drugs that would keep my body and mind in balance. At least for now, as Parkinson's symptoms are mercurial and today's balance is tomorrow's rollercoaster.

Back to my informal little group of five, four whose role was understood and me. A patient, for sure, but also I am a nurse with more than thirty years of experience, working in hospitals.

For years I had been a night supervisor whose units included the Psychiatric Services. I had delivered my first baby on Psych. A young addict had gone into premature labor and I arrived first after the nurses' emergency page. By the time the OB resident found the unit, the little one was atop its girl-mom's belly.

I know hospitals. I know people. I know myself. Two of my truisms have long been, 'Do your best every day' and 'Thinking ahead as to how the present will be remembered gives the strength to make decisions and the courage to take risks.' It was time to turn my Hallmarky platitudes into Weaver strategy.

'Will there be a meeting tonight?' I inquired.

'Yes,' the nurse replied. 'I'm conducting it. Maybe we'll do karaoke.'

Karaoke. Just a word, that's all it took to spark my spirit. I can't sing but I write and I love music. Back in Bethany, Friday night means Simple Truth at the Cottage Café and I had heard Aaron would be singing at the Fat Tuna. I'd have had to split my evening out if I had been home. Music, the common denominator of joyful expression throughout the world. With music, even the speechless can sing.

I walked into the day room. Only two patients were there, both schitzies, but doing well that day. The voices were quiet and non-threatening. Within twenty feet of the other, each was alone. 'We're going to sing tonight,' I said, sitting where I could interact with both. 'Karaoke at the community meeting. Let's practice.'

'I bet you can sing,' I said to one. And he started to sing, a Michael Jackson tune with high pitched lilting tones. He finished and the other stood up and started his own song, a Marvin Gaye ballad.

It was amazing, wondrous. Two men I had only heard mutter a few disconnected words were singing whole songs, beautifully. First one and then the other, each minded the other's space. The day room nurse got involved and the four of us enjoyed an early snack.

Then the elevator door opened and the addicts returned from their Friday NA meeting. The room filled. It would soon be time for the 9:00 PM community meeting. The incongruity of the moment struck me. I started to write a verse that could be sung, using a beat I had already used for one of my poems. It started, 'Feeling good, got the rhythm...Friday night, hell of a situation...'

I turned to one of the men who had just sung. 'Hear this rhythm,' I asked, humming my song. 'Can you scat for me?' He knew what I meant and Ella Fitzgerald smiled on us! I asked the nurse if I could speak at the end of the meeting.

The idea of the community meeting is to make sure that all the patients have the opportunity to bring up issues with the rest of the community or about the environment that can be readily dealt with. The biggest complaint is always the food but that appears to be an insolvable problem. Before moving on to karaoke, the nurse turned to me. 'Mrs. Weaver...' she invited.

I looked around. There were about twenty of us, patients and staff. 'I've written a little song for us before karaoke,' I said. 'but I need help with the rhythm...please join in.'

And they did. They clapped their hands with the beat, swayed with the rhythm and repeated a couple of phrases, 'hell of a situation...hell of a situation.' There was a moment of silence. Then we all laughed. Do you hear? We laughed. It was the first laughter I had heard all week.

The magic continued. The two men who had first started to sing before the meeting sang again for the group. Three other patients followed them. Each stood up and with karaoke mic in hand, sang a cappella, and smiled with pride and pleasure at the sound of inevitable applause. And then the whole group, staff and patients alike, sang corny old karaoke songs like 'Home, home on the range.' Even the silent ones. 'Home, home, home...' sang one, his hands clapping the plastic tray of his wheelchair, his face for once relaxed.

For twenty brief minutes, we were all we, merely human beings making the best of a trying time. An indigestible day ended with a strawberry milkshake nightcap.

* * *

I hung up the phone satisfied with myself. It was time for dinner so I walked in the day room and found my tray in the cart. I sat next to a tall thin dark-skinned man named Joe. He told me that he was an addict in his twenties, had been clean for ten years but had gone back to using after a back injury. I noticed that he walked with his back bent forward and his left hand supporting the lumbar area. "My mattress here is a killer," he explained, "and I'm not allowed pain medicine. I don't know how I'm goin' to make it."

On this occasion we both complained to each other that once again the kitchen messed up our menu. Joe didn't get his chocolate milk and I got ice cream instead of cake. It sounds silly but when you're locked in, food is one of the few things to look forward to.

"Mrs. Weaver, telephone in the hallway," someone yelled.

It was Greg. "Mum, Lauren was hoping you were going to wish her happy birthday."

Oh my God. I had forgotten.

That evening I couldn't sleep. For the first time in my life, I wondered about how I could kill myself. I got up from my bed, removed the draw string belt from my purple and blue striped pants, fashioned a noose around the shower head and pulled on it as hard as I could. It could hold my weight, I decided.

I was scared. It was the first time I had actively thought of a means to kill myself.

I walked out of my room, down the dimly lit corridor to the nurses' station. "I'm afraid. I've been thinking about suicide" I told the charge nurse. "Please may I talk to my family?"

"No, it's not allowed at this time of night," she replied.

I begged her to please let me call Kim. "She's a nurse, like you. Like I was."

"No, you're not allowed to call out until after breakfast. That's the rule."

I screamed aloud in the corridor before being hustled away into seclusion. It was a scream louder than any sound has ever risen from my throat, and it reverberated down the light-dimmed, barren corridor like the trumpet from an elephant caged in the Large Animal House at the zoo.

The next day I apologized to my fellow patients if I woke any of them up. Several put their arm around my shoulder or gave me a thumb's up. They understood.

I was put on suicide precautions. This meant my room was located nearer the nurses' station and someone had to watch me at all times.

"I can't stand these Blue patients," a big man wearing the standard white scrub suit of psychiatric technicians grumbled to a colleague the following night. He made no effort to prevent my hearing his words. I was nobody to him, just another nuisance Blue team crazy.

He drew up a second chair to rest his feet on, as he sat outside my room, noisily turning every page of every newspaper patients, visitors and staff left behind on the unit. I couldn't sleep with the light from the corridor penetrating through my half-opened door and the sound of his chatter to whomever came past.

A lovely nurse from Nigeria came in to give me my meds. I was trying to write a poem about meditation to help me relax and refocus my attention from the decidedly uncaring care-taker, supposedly watching my every move.

Her voice was lilting from her African dialect and comfortably English from her British schooling. She worked as many extra shifts as she could so that she would have the money to bring her children to join her in America. She helped me write the verse that was repeated throughout my long, calming poem:

> *Gee egwu. Gee egwu,*
> *Listen, music.*
> *Ma mara ihe egwu ua ada,*
> *Feel rhythm.*
> *Nuru okwu nice obi,*
> *Hear the language of souls.*
> *Gee egwu. Gee egwu.*

Four days later, Dr. Leo discharged me with instructions to return to see him in three weeks. Then, his nurse called. Dr. Leo would be going on vacation so my return appointment had been postponed from June to August. Strange, I thought, but who was I to question?

"Let us go on vacation, too," I said to Ike. "There's a conference in Berkeley about stem cell research, I'd like to attend."

The conference was the first national meeting of the Stem Cell Action Network. Both Ike and I learned so much. We sat at round tables which had been placed far enough apart to accommodate the wheelchairs, walkers, and portable ventilators of people with spinal chord injuries, multiple sclerosis, and Parkinson's. One morning, to our right was a family with children with diabetes and to our left were a mother and her twenty-six year old son. She became his caregiver when he became paralyzed from a surfing accident at age eighteen.

Together, in rapt attention, we watched Christopher Reeve talk to us from a large screen. Together, we shared tissues and hope.

It was in Berkeley, I heard the phrase, "Think Clone, Think Cure".

We flew home on a red-eye. A couple of years ago I would have bounced back but I couldn't get over feeling overwhelmingly tired.

I called Dr. Leo four times requesting help. "I'm exhausted. I have no energy and I've got so much to do," I'd complain.

"Take all your meds on time, including the Celexa (anti depressant) and take an additional regular Sinemet on top of the CR (controlled release) whenever you need it. You've got to let the Sinemet kick back in after San Francisco" was always the answer. "While I'm on vacation, you can call Dr. Fielding who'll be back next week from a conference in Europe," he added the last time.

At five in the morning, the Saturday before Father's Day, and the day Dr. Leo was to leave for vacation, I sent him an email and cc'd Dr. Fielding. It said:

Christina Weaver

"Greetings

Per discussion with Dr. Leo, I started to take Tasmar tid starting yesterday Friday in addition to 2 extra Sinemet regulars...

Through yesterday, I remained awake but thinking sluggishly. For the first time this morning, I awoke early of my own accord (before 9:00AM) and am thinking better. We shall see...

Thanks for your concern.
Christina"

13

Trust Lost

An email at dawn, a bummer of a day, a tattoo, an unhappy family, Father's Day tomorrow, "I might as well go to bed too," I told Ike who was sitting on his corner of the couch where he watched TV every evening.

"Right," he sighed again.

But all was not right.

And the night was far from over.

* * *

I rested my head against the back seat of the state trooper's car, and fingered the stretched skin at the sides of my neck where staples and sutures held taut the two inch jagged cuts. I felt no pain.

But then it hadn't hurt when two evenings earlier, Father's Day eve, I kept digging the razor blades, one in each hand, as deep as I could along the pulsating course of my carotid arteries in my neck and my femoral arteries in my groin. Just as it hadn't hurt when earlier that same day my right wrist was tattooed with the words "Think Clone, Think Cure."

Nothing hurt except for the overwhelming sense that I was in over my head and had committed myself to doing more than there were minutes in the day. And I was so tired, so tired. So tired, that about two minutes after our son and daughter and their families departed for their vacation cottage nearby, I kissed Ike good night and got ready for bed. It was about nine o'clock.

In the bathroom, I looked in my four compartment daily pillbox and realized I had forgotten to take my five o'clock meds. So I swallowed: a Sinemet CR, an additional Sinemet regular, as Dr. Leo advised when I wasn't feeling well, a Tasmar, an Aricept (an Alzheimer's drug that my doctors thought might help with cognition problems in Parkinson's), and a Celexa, an anti-depressant. This was my routine.

I lay down on my side of the double bed and looked at the ceiling. Exhaustion and panic enveloped me. "How am I ever going to be able to do all the things I had promised people I would do the next day?"

I was like the proverbial man on the train "going round and round, 'neath the streets of Boston", who couldn't get off. I couldn't get off. I was so tired, so tired yet I couldn't go to sleep.

And, then it struck me, totally out of the blue. "It would be easier to be dead. Just kill yourself. Get it over." And then I rationalized, "Actually it's a great time to off myself. Everyone's here, they'11 be able to support each other and they'11 realize that this is best in the long run for us all."

It didn't occur to me to reach over and slide open the door of the headboard where Ike kept the hunting knife since before the first time I had first snuggled next to him in 1964. I didn't think to go in the next room where the extra sharp double edge blades I use to cut my mat board lay in their place. If it had been planned, I would have succeeded. "Planning is the key to success," my Dad had told me when, as an eight-year old English schoolgirl, I started a class project collecting wild flowers. Like most of his words of wisdom, I had taken the adage to heart.

Focused, I got up and went to the bathroom. I looked at my pills and then next to them, the injector razor I shave my legs with. Picking it up, I wondered how to use it to cut myself deep enough. Then, I looked in the cabinet and saw the packet of razor blades. I took two out and put the packet back.

Then I opened the medication cupboard and saw a bottle of Tylenol. That will work as a backup, I thought as I emptied the dozen or so into the palm of my hand and swallowed them with the same glass of water I had taken my Parkie pills.

I took my nightdress off and put it in the hamper. There was no need for it to get soiled after all, and I lay naked between the pink, blue and aqua colored, abstract designed sheets.

I held one blade between my thumb and first finger in each hand and felt with my fingertips for the pulses of arteries that were my target. I dug them both at the same time into either side of my neck.

It didn't hurt but it didn't result in much blood either So, I cut again and again.

And then I decided I wasn't bleeding enough so I attacked each side of my groin. Fascinated by the spurts, oozes and sweet smell of my own blood as it dripped down my neck and thighs before forming large soft clots, I became aware of our two pets.

Jasmine, our cat of thirteen years, had been disturbed from her spot on the chair. She jumped on the bed and I felt her whiskers brush my cheek as she sniffed my neck. Then she leapt toward the door and started scratching it violently. But her efforts were in vain. The TV was on and I knew Ike wouldn't hear her.

Our five-month old cockapoo puppy, Topper, on the other hand, tried to snuggle closer and closer to my body. I kept him on top of the covers, not wanting his short white curly fur to be stained by his soon-to-be-dead mistress' blood. That would be distressing to the family, I thought.

Then it dawned on me, "Finding me like this is going to be pretty upsetting for Ike. I shouldn't let him find me when he is by himself." I stretched over and picked up the phone and dialed 411 for information.

"Could you forward me to the non-emergency number for the state police?" I asked.

"Yes, it's not an emergency. I don't need anyone to get here too fast, I just want an officer to come to my home," I told the voice who answered. When you have an English accent and sound like you know what you're talking about, people don't question you much, I've found.

I lay back. Well I've done my best to make this as easy as possible for them, I thought. Time to start cutting again.

Damn these blades get blunt quickly. I pushed one in so far and hard it even bent. My thinking was getting blurry. That was good, about time to show signs of lack of oxygen to my brain.

I laid one of the blades on my chest and pushed my right index finger deep into the hole in my groin. Then I turned over and tried to write in capital letters on Ike's pillow. "I love you all. Don't blame yourselves. This is best."

My scribble was never noticed. I wanted to write who I wanted to have what and wished I'd given more thought to unfinished business before I started cutting. I hadn't even paid some of the bills that were due. That wasn't like me.

The blood had felt warm as it pooled around my body but I started to feel cool. Topper felt me shiver and moved even closer.

The door opened and Ike came into the bedroom. Shoot, I'm still alive and where's that darn policeman?

I closed my eyes, pretending to be asleep, listening to his movement around the side of the bed. I heard him gasp and then a strangled moan as he tore the covers from my neck.

"What have you done? What have you done? Oh God, God."

I'll never forget how his face sagged. His eyes had grown round and deep and they glistened like muddy fishing holes in the stark glare of the bedside lamp as he tried to take in the scene before him. If you were asked to draw a picture of bewilderment it was Ike's face.

"Let me die," I begged him, reaching out to touch his hand. "It won't take much longer. Go back and watch TV."

But he wouldn't; he couldn't. After he dialed 911, I helped him call the number where out kids were staying. His fingers, normally carpenter-steady, were desperately pushing and missing buttons on the cell phone. I couldn't just lie there watching him struggle. We had always worked together. But my body had grown heavy and my mind effervescent, so I just lay there and stared at the little chain dangling beneath the whirring blades of the ceiling fan. It rotated counter clockwise.

"Look at her eyes, she's wild. She's out of her mind. That's not her. That's not her in that bed," I heard Ike repeat to the officer who rushed up the stairs when, by now, he had received the second, now emergency, call to come to our home.

* * *

Pandemonium surrounded me. There was Ike, a retired psychiatric social worker; Greg, our thirty-four year old son, who manages computer systems; Kim, who was thirty-one and a head nurse on a cardiology unit; Stan her husband, a doctor whose specialty is pediatric emergency medicine, two police officers, six firemen, eventually three medics, and Topper, who wouldn't stop yapping even when he was closed behind the door of an adjacent room.

Flashes of conversation hit me. "Greg, give me your belt," said Stan trying to fashion a tourniquet. "Greg, find me some shoes," said Kim who had run to the house barefoot. (He found her white nursing shoes in the back of her car and she wore them with the beach attire she was still wearing. "I don't know, they seemed appropriate," he explained later).

"Hey Slim, hold the IV," said one of the Medics to Kim. (Later, Stan and I found out that he had worked with her at the Washington Hospital Center and that was her nickname).

"I'm praying for you," called out Stan, the only religious one of us, as I was carried on the stretcher from the bedroom. I tried to yell back, "Stan, I still don't get it, no tunnel of light" but the oxygen mask over my nose and mouth smothered my words and my thoughts switched elsewhere.

The ambulance flew at full speed, siren blasting, from our home fifteen miles south. I was exsanguinating before the medics' eyes. "You'll be alright, just relax", one tried to reassure me as she watched my blood pressure sink and the blood seep through the pressure bandages.

But I kept wiggling and moving as much as I could, trying to pump out the last spurt of blood from congealing blood vessels.

"Please Mum, don't die," Kim pleaded from her position behind my head at the back of the ambulance. She stroked my hair with her hands and tears but I was in a world of frenzy.

I hate failure.

* * *

I stayed in the ER long enough for the doctor to make another incision in my neck, it's called a cut-down, to get to a blood vessel for IV fluids to run into. As he pressed down the one-inch paper tape to cover the wound, I reached up and ripped out the tubing along with his carefully knotted stitches.

If looks could kill, suicide would have been unnecessary. He was furious at me. I just looked at him and said, "Don't take it personally; I am trying to kill myself you know." What a smart ass, I could imagine him thinking!

My stretcher was pushed into the Operating Room and anesthesia gave peace to us both. From the time I woke up until I was judged to be medically stable and was sent on my merry way up north as fast as the hospital could make the arrangements, my wrists and ankles were held in place by leather restraints. I understood. Not only had I been a nurse but the hospital where I had been vice president was very similar in size and type.

Suicidal patients are time consuming and costly to the hospital, scary to nurses used to caring for bodies not minds, and in this day and age, a legal liability, to boot. A court official came to the hospital and judged me to be actively suicidal so I was to be transferred to the nearest psychiatric hospital with an available bed.

* * *

"Don't trust her. You can't trust her no matter what she says. She's just not herself."

I was furious. How dare he talk about me that way? And how can he let them drive me away, alone, at eleven o'clock at night?

I was sitting in the back of a police car. It was the kind that has a thick glass barrier between the officers in the front and the poor wretch in the back. I remember it smelled of new leather and was pristine clean.

Ike was talking to two Delaware state troopers. I couldn't see him but his voice sounded flat, tired and old; a voice that normally resonated with a rich deep baritone sound and a hint of black DC. Ike's voice has made people ask if he used to be in radio.

"She's had Parkinson's for ten years, you said? Don't worry, we'll look after her," one of the troopers replied. He had the air of self-confidence garnered from height, years in the field, and a gun on his hip. He added, "My grandfather died of it. Doesn't want to be a burden, I'll bet, I understand what she's going through."

I later found out the two were off duty detectives who had volunteered for the extra duty at the end of their regular shift. They probably thought it would be an easy way to make some extra money.

"Here's a pillow for her so she can lie down and be comfortable." It was a nurse's voice I heard. She must have felt sorry for me. Emergency room nurses are a hardened bunch, but seeing one of their own, a former nurse, with a progressively deteriorating illness and self inflicted deep wounds down both sides of her neck and groin being forced in the back of a squad car, struck a chord.

One of the officers opened the car door and gave me the pillow. I thanked him, put it next to me on the seat and stared straight ahead. I don't remember if Ike said goodbye. I know I didn't say anything to him.

The engine started and we drove away from the garishly bright lights of the emergency room ambulance bay at Beebe Hospital in Lewes, Delaware. We were headed north towards the unknown of a Psychiatric Hospital, an hour and a half's drive away.

I waited until we had picked up speed on Route 1 before reaching out to test the handle of the car door.

I touched it gingerly, half thinking it might be wired to detect someone trying to open it. And then I pushed the handle down as hard as I could. Damn, as expected, the door was locked so hurling my body on to the highway wasn't an option.

The officers took no notice. They were looking at the road ahead, talking, although I couldn't hear any words. I pulled the pillow on my lap, mind still galloping, wondering what to do next.

With my head back and the pillow in my lap, I reviewed my options. I wondered if the pillowcase was long enough to make into a noose. Staying as still as possible so as not to attract attention from the front seat, I slipped the pillowcase off the plastic bag that covered the brand new pillow. Yes a plastic bag, there for the suffocating! I lay down across the seat, pulled open the plastic bag, lay the pillowcase on top of the pillow, covered my head with the plastic bag, pulled it tight around my neck and started breathing deeply.

I heard the squeal of breaks at the same time as the sudden stop rolled me off the seat onto the floor. Almost as quickly, the door opened and the plastic bag was yanked away from my face.

"I'm sorry but we are going to have to handcuff you."

"I understand," I replied. "You have your job to do."

With my hands locked behind my back, I felt like the prisoner I was; a prisoner who, in my mind, had committed no crime.

My mind raced back to the era of the sixties when I first came to America and people were being arrested in civil rights protests. And then I thought of the anti Vietnam War peace demonstrations of the seventies. I recalled the passive resistance tactics I had watched on TV and decided that when we arrived at the hospital I would go limp.

I wasn't going to walk in there as though I was a volunteer. With one officer pulling me from one side of the car, and the other pushing from the other side, I was like a sack of potatoes. They were huffing and puffing and twisting their torsos to get me out.

"Wait," I said and they stopped momentarily. "Look, it's me I want to hurt, not you. Don't injure your backs on my account." Then I regained my dead weight position. Ghandi and King would be proud, I thought.

When they eventually got me into the awaiting wheel chair, I heard the officer whose grandfather had Parkinson's tell the night nursing supervisor, "Her medications are in this bag. We were told to make sure we inform you that she should stay on her current regime." Then he uncuffed me, shook my hand and wished me good luck. I was lucky it was compassionate professionals who volunteered to "do transport" that evening.

* * *

My accommodations were designed for functionality. I was in a room large enough to permit a twelve-inch perimeter of bare floor around a single bed size, white sheeted, slippery, hard-as-nails-in-a-coffin mattress. The walls were windowless and stark and the door, which opened into the central locked nurses' quarters, remained open so I could be under constant watch. A toilet with a hand basin was adjacent and its door also was required to remain open. Somehow its echo made the mere hint of an expression of flatulence travel with the resonance of a boom box's deepest bass.

It was in this room, two sleepless days after my admission and continuing deep conviction that I would be better off dead that I was jolted back to being me. I had returned from a meeting with the psychiatrist who had been on call when I arrived, and Ike, Greg and Kim. "You're going to be a hard case to crack," he had told me after our first interview.

I hadn't cried, or got angry, or asked for special favors. "Don't worry, I won't try it again here, not while you're watching me. That wouldn't be sensible and sure, I'll continue to take my Parkinson's meds," I assured him.

"You may need to be hospitalized for a long time," he responded.

The meeting with my family and the doctor hadn't gone well. We sat on upright chairs crowded into another small windowless room that a different psychiatrist each month used as his office. I looked in my lap and at the doctor for the entire meeting.

"It's hard for you to understand but I really believe in the long run, you'll appreciate why it's better for me to die now before I get to be a burden," I repeated to my family, like the inanimate voice at airports, reminding one to keep one's possessions under our own control.

"But we love you, Mum. We want you around however bad you'll get." I heard the pain in their voices but it didn't penetrate my shell of resistance. I walked away from the doctor's office and lay down in my cell with the sheet over my head.

I hoped they wouldn't follow me. But they did. "I'm sorry, you're not allowed in the Quiet Room," I heard a nurse telling them. They took no notice.

I felt Kim's body fall on top of mine, clinging to me like ivy to a trap door of an old root cellar. She was sobbing. I felt the desperation in her red, swollen eyes and my heart of stone crumbled. As quickly as the switch to self-destruct had turned on, it shut down.

The thought, "What am I doing to my daughter, my beloved baby?" flashed through my befuddled brain. I was killing her, not me. I looked up into my son's contorted face, trying so hard to remain composed.

"It's over," I told him. "I won't try it again. I need to live. *I* see that now, I promise." I meant it. Greg nodded. Our eyes and minds had connected.

It would take Ike a long time to trust me again.

"You must leave," the nurse insisted.

"Come on, Kim. You can't stay," said Ike, reaching down to wrench Kim's grip away from me. "We'll come back tomorrow," he told the nurse.

* * *

Ike knew the rules. He had placed many patients in seclusion, as it used to be termed, when he worked at Saint Elizabeth's. And he knew not to believe what most patients said after they had been locked away for a few days, no matter how earnest they sounded.

Ike didn't trust me and I didn't trust myself either.

I kept wondering why on earth I tried to kill myself. I hadn't been depressed and I certainly hadn't planned it.

The night nurse observed me still awake and invited me out of my cell to the Day Room for a chat. "I heard your family came to visit," she probed.

"Yes, and I expect you heard in report that I'm no longer suicidal," I replied.

"Not suicidal," she restated in her best psychiatric nurse, I-know-better-than-to-agree fashion.

"I'm afraid I'm going out of my mind," I bubbled, needing to confide. "You know, I promised my family I'd never try to kill myself again. And I mean it. But I hadn't intended to commit suicide the night I tried. It just happened. And I thought with such certainty it was the right thing to do.

"You know, I think I understand the mind of the criminally insane. Maybe their brains get so twisted, like mine was, that they convince themselves to do evil things for reasons that seem so logically right at the time. What if that feeling should come over me again?

"It's not like I got depressed beforehand and could tell someone I needed help. That's why I don't feel guilty. It was as though I didn't do it, as though it was a different mind functioning in my head. Maybe I'm becoming schizophrenic. Maybe it's my Parkinson's meds. I'd prefer to be stiff and shaky than not be able to trust myself."

The nurse put her arm around me as though waiting for me to cry. Her skin smelt of lily of the valley and her long hair rubbed against my cheek and brushed my stitches. I've never been the touchy-feely type and I wasn't ready to deal with sympathy. After a while she brought me a cup of tea that brought an English stiff upper lip smile to my face.

"You know I've already written a memoir," I told her. "But this wasn't the way it ended."

"Maybe you'll have a new beginning," she smiled.

Later I saw her get my chart and start writing. There is no such thing as a private conversation when you're on a psych unit.

It's a disconcerting thing about trust, you don't think about it until it has been shaken. Who could have known that it was misplaced trust in those whose oath is never to harm that had so changed our lives?

14

Duped by Dopamine

My family had been convinced to get me re-admitted to the medical center where my history was known. I didn't want to go. Frankly I felt scared to be back on the Blue team.

After four years in his research program and under his psychiatric care, I no longer trusted Dr. Leo. Somehow I knew my meds were part of my problem and certainly the last hospitalization hadn't helped. I was scared to go back because I wasn't sure I could play the game this time. I wasn't sure that I'd ever be able to land on Home again.

Dr. Fielding was becoming my star of hope. Like Dr. Leo, he was a Parkinson's specialist, but he was a neurologist, not a psychiatrist. Dr. Fielding had recently come to the medical center and I was one of his first patients. He was in his early thirties and had been recruited by the medical center after a fellowship in movement disorders from a prestigious New England academic medical center.

From the first time I saw him, Dr. Fielding indicated some doubt about my Parkinson's diagnosis. In fact on my next visit to Dr. Leo, a lot of blood tests were ordered as well as an MRI of my brain. Two results were noteworthy: The MRI showed I had a small stroke at some time in the past, and the blood work revealed hyperhomocysteinemia.

Dr. Fielding told me that studies were showing that this abnormality was being associated with people taking Parkinson's meds and that this could have been the cause of the stroke. He prescribed Folic Acid to decrease the level of homocysteine. Later he printed out for me an article from his computer entitled, *"Elevated Plasma Homocysteine Level in Patients with Parkinson's Disease"*. Dr. Fielding told me that he thought hyperhomocysteinemia was the main culprit behind a lot of my memory and other cognition problems.

After his suspicions, my diagnosis on my medical record at the medical center was changed from Parkinson's disease to Parkinsonism. However, no changes were made in my regime of meds.

The term, "Parkinsonism" is used, one doctor told me later, when the specific cause of the disease is known, like a chemical toxicity. "Not like your situation," he added. Another physician said that an "ism" label gets attached when doctors don't really know what is going on.

Kim talked to both Dr. Leo, who was reached on vacation, and Dr. Fielding about getting me re-admitted to the medical center. Dr. Leo by now was saying I must have bipolar illness and that my family may want to consider electro-convulsive (shock) therapy. Kim knew better than to tell me that. Dr. Fielding promised he would come and see me every day. It is because of Dr. Fielding, I agreed that Ike and Kim could drive me back there.

* * *

For the first few days back at the medical center, I slept. Dr. Fielding came to see me every day as he promised. On the fourth day he told me something exciting, something that gave me hope.

"I want you to spend the day with me tomorrow in my outpatient clinic. I want to video you at different times in relation to your meds."

Dr. Leo who was now back from vacation, opposed this idea. "I'll get the resident to photograph her here on Psych, if necessary," he said. "She can't be allowed in an unsecured area and we don't have the staff to stay with her."

But Dr. Fielding prevailed against his superiors in this classically hierarchical organization, and arrangements were made. I promised that I would call back to the unit every hour on the cell phone Greg lent me.

No problem! I was delighted to prove that I wouldn't try to escape, let Dr. Fielding down, or worse. I also couldn't wait to have time to be alone, time to experience warm, humid un-air conditioned air, and time to savor the tall cafe mocha I could purchase from the vendor in the lobby!

June 30, 2004 is as significant a day in my life as November 22, 1963 and September 11ᵗʰ, 2001 is to America.

I awoke early and spent some time thinking about what to wear. After all I was being videotaped!

There wasn't much choice of attire. I was naked when I left home last and Ike packed a distinctly motley variety of clothes in my overnight wheels. I ended up with a white tee-shirt and a green button-down-the-front, long dress. The dress was chosen as a sign of defiance as despite my being on a suicide watch nobody had noticed that the dress had a thin but strong tie-in-the-back string that could have made an effective hanging device.

To complete my ensemble I wore the only shoes that Ike had brought. They were bright red, soft leather, Moroccan slip-ons with a high back. I remember looking in the mirror and seeing the jagged wounds down both sides of my neck, still held together by sutures, staples and paper tape. What does it matter what I'm wearing? It's my neck people will look at, I thought.

The attendant wheeled me to the clinic at eight o'clock. I had taken my morning pills already. I took my next four pills again at eleven. As the day progressed, it became obvious to both Dr. Fielding and me that the longer I was off my meds, the better I did.

On the last segment of the tape, Dr Fielding asked what I thought. I looked into the camera and read the words I had written during the previous hour of waiting and thinking in the outside corridor:

> *Doped for years*
> *Dopey for a week*
> *Doped up for an hour*
> *Duped by dopamine,*
> *Indebted to Dr. Fielding*

"Paradoxical" was the word I saw Dr. Fielding write in his notes about the relationship of the Parkinson's medications to the way my body reacted.

Together, we looked into the viewfinder of his camera to review the day's video snapshots of time. It was amazing then, and remains so each time I look at the souvenir copy of the CD he later gave me.

I saw how badly I looked around noon, shortly after taking my last meds. I saw the jerky tapping on the floor of my incongruously red shoes. I observed my gait so awkward that I looked drunk and how I lost my balance and almost fell over as an assistant gave me a slight pull backwards. I watched my struggle through yawns and grimaces to touch my nose with my forefinger and turn the palms of my hands up and down.

But at the end of the day, I looked so smooth!

Shoot, I almost looked normal! It was 6:30 PM when Dr. Fielding and I walked back to the unit. We chatted about our families and talked about the struggle in academic medical centers to get the funding required to do research. "I've always wanted to make a difference for people dealing with the every day problems of chronic movement disorders. I didn't realize I'd have to spend so much time giving speeches and marketing myself instead of doing the work," he told me.

"Back to the lock up!" he joked conspiratorially when we rang the bell to get admission to the unit. Unlike the psychiatrists, he didn't have a key either. I signed myself back in and made a point of telling the nurse who sat in the glass barricaded nurses' station, "I'm back."

"Let's see how you are tomorrow morning," Dr. Fielding said cautiously. "And I'll put all your meds on hold for tonight."

* * *

I got back on the unit just in time to get my first visitors, other than my family: my *lower case blues* boys! They came in the day room slowly, looking around warily at my fellow patients. Several patients stared back, surprised to see my young, handsome visitors, dressed in jeans and black tee-shirts and with arms opened wide to hug me.

Before I even said hi, I blurted out, "I think I found out today I don't have Parkinson's."

"No kidding?" said B.J. the bass player who had read my entire *Third Wheel* manuscript.

My cheerful demeanor wasn't what they expected to find. After all, they came to show their support to a friend whose out-of-the-blue suicide attempt they couldn't understand. Instead, found me smiling like a deluded fool.

"This is so weird," commented Paul, the drummer. No kidding!

* * *

The next day, Dr. Fielding arrived early on the unit. We repeated the series of neuro tests that had consumed yesterday and both agreed that indeed my physical movements were, in fact, even smoother and my mind even clearer. He spent a long time writing his findings in my chart. This time he formally discontinued all my meds; no more Parkinson's meds and no more antidepressants, cold turkey.

Later one of the residents said Dr. Leo would meet me in the afternoon. I called Ike, Greg and Kim to join us.

The meeting was conducted in the bedroom I shared with another patient who kindly agreed to leave us alone.

After my family, the first to arrive were the incoming and outgoing psych residents (for it was July 1st, the infamous day in hospitals when the year moves on for young doctors).

"Have you heard?" the outgoing resident mentioned to her successor, "Mrs. Weaver doesn't have Parkinson's."

Greg heard her too and turned to smile at me. Kim and I were sitting sideways on my bed with our backs to the wall. I felt her hand reach over and give mine a squeeze. It was the first time we had heard from a professional what we felt to be true.

It was a quick meeting. Dr. Leo sat forward on the edge of his chair. It was the one armchair in the room and it had been left deferentially for him. My chart was in his lap and sometimes he rested his elbows on it, cradling his chin in the white knuckles of his hands. He acknowledged that he'd read Dr. Fielding's progress note but that he hadn't had time to return his call.

He refused to consider the possibility that not only did I not have Parkinson's but that in fact all my psychiatric and cognitive symptoms could possibly be related to my Parkinson's' meds. He didn't say he was sorry.

Our exchange became antagonistic and the residents glanced uncomfortably at each other. This wasn't the way text books described the physician-patient dynamic. Dr. Leo indicated he would be taking a long 4th of July holiday weekend and recommended that I stay hospitalized until he returned. It's not just his last words to us that I remember so vividly; it was his avoidance of our eyes and his tone of defiance.

"I still want your brain for the study," he said.

It's strange how flashes from the past pop into your mind, "*Illegitimati non ...*"

No way, not me!

* * *

It didn't take long for the news of my situation to spread around the unit. For one thing, I couldn't keep a big grin off my face. To know I didn't have Parkinson's and, as far as I was concerned, wasn't mentally ill, was such an amazing burden lifted from my shoulders.

My fellow patients reacted as though a minor miracle had occurred. "Praise the Lord," many said.

"When you write your book about all this, please don't mention my name," asked the outgoing resident. "I'm a private person and I know you're a writer."

"I used to be a private person, too," I told her.

Greg and Lauren came to see me on Independence Day morning. By then the new attending psychiatrist could see no need for my continued hospitalization. He and Greg talked and they agreed it was time for me to be discharged.

"Does my Mum need any prescriptions?" I heard Greg ask.

"Actually, no," the doctor responded. "I'll tell Dr. Leo."

When the nurse locked the door behind us and we got into the elevator, the three of us hugged. Lauren really didn't know what was going on but she knew it was a time to be joyous.

"Free at last, thank God almighty, free at last," I exalted.

"Un-fucking-believable," Greg mouthed above Lauren's head, accentuating each syllable. How right he was!

We arrived at Greg and Liz' house on Main Street, small-town Virginia, just in time for the July 4th Parade. The whole family gathered on the curb, sitting on fold-up beach chairs and waving our little stars and stripes. Ike and I sat next to each other and held hands. Aged four, two and one, our little granddaughters, squealing with delight, darted to the side of the street to pick up pieces of candy that were tossed to them from passing floats.

Tears of relief and gratitude pricked my eyes when sirens wailed from ambulances, fire engines and police cars. My happy grin was still firmly entrenched. I'm even smiling as I write about it, a couple of years later!

16

Freed to be Flawed

Michael J. Fox called his book, *Lucky Man*. Now I understand why. When he was an actor, he affected people through the characters he played. Now, as a Parkie and an advocate for stem cell research, he effects change by his very character. And he has met and changed the lives of people whose paths he likely would not have crossed before his diagnosis.

I, too, am lucky.

* * *

It was amazing how quickly my psyche started to return to normal. Back in February 2004, when my elderly cousin, Pat, in England became ill, I asked Greg to accompany me. I was afraid I'd get confused in the airport. I worried I'd spend too much money. (It didn't help. I still managed to buy a couple of thousand dollars worth of art when he wasn't with me.) But mostly, I was concerned that I'd blurt out something inappropriate.

She got ill again in August, about a month after my discharge. I felt comfortable enough to travel alone. More important, Ike felt comfortable to let me out of his protective sight. And a month later when I had to return a third time, I even felt mentally up to hiring a car and driving around London.

"You're almost back to your old self," she observed. "Your Dad would have been so happy."

How ironic. My Dad died prematurely because he couldn't deal with the idea of watching my decline with Parkinson's. My not being able to read bothered him the most. He took advantage of a bad case of influenza on top of his emphysema, didn't tell anybody until he collapsed, and then refused anything to eat or drink. It took him seven long days to dehydrate and die. I was with him in the hospital the whole time.

"He loved you too much," Pat said at the time.

* * *

What a relief it is go from 20 to three pills a day. I continue to take Folic Acid to keep the homocysteine level within normal limits as well as a baby aspirin to help prevent another stroke. Also, I take glucosamine to ease the pains from the arthritis that has made its presence known. (Apparently my arthritic symptoms were masked by the anti-inflammatory side effects of the Parkinson's drugs).

Dr. Fielding was told that before he could see me again, Dr. Leo insisted I must be under the care of a psychiatrist. I complied and saw one who is recognized for his expertise in the area of pharmaceuticals and psychiatric disorders. He never saw a need to prescribe any kind of medications because, as he said, "I see no signs of mental illness."

Increasing toxicity from years of taking anti-Parkinson's and anti-depressant drugs while having neither Parkinson's nor clinical depression is, he believes, the sole cause of my behavioral change.

* * *

I expected to feel immediately like my "Before Parkinson's" self. But I don't. Worst is the long-term brain damage that has affected my memory and ability to learn new things. Thank goodness that while I was taking the meds I became such a prolific writer.

In fact, it is only the things I wrote about that I remember clearly – not the births of my granddaughters or the deaths of two pets, nor family visits, nor holiday celebrations, nor vacations, nor the hospitalizations when I injured my back, nor the mundane. I used to be a news junky and now I find out that in 2003 there was a shuttle disaster and in Afghanistan there was a war that totally eluded me. I don't yet know what else I never knew or just don't remember.

People who were close friends tell me they stopped visiting and inviting us to their homes because all I could talk about was me. "I'd spend hours fixing a great supper and you wouldn't even sit down to eat, you'd be so keen on reading your latest masterpiece," said one.

"And she's a great cook," noted Ike, bemoaning the break in dinner invitations!

It's odd to realize others perceived me so differently than I saw myself.

Not too long ago, I got a call from one of my musician friends. Ike and I befriended his teenage daughter and I took her for a sightseeing couple of days in Washington, DC while we stayed with Kim's family.

"She won't be able to do that again," her father explained. "My ex found out and is using the fact that I allowed her to be with someone she considers immoral, as a factor in our custody fight. Suicide is a sin, you know."

Similarly, another individual warned me I would never enter the gates of heaven as attempting suicide is "an affront to God." Yet another with concerns about my after life, fussed at me for defiling my body by getting my arm tattooed.

In a different light, I walked into Happy Harry's drug store one day and realized that a man was walking towards me and pointing me out to his companion. "You're the one, aren't you? The one who wrote in the paper about going into a mental hospital?" I nodded and he put his arm around me. "Thanks so much. That was a brave thing to do," he exclaimed. "You caused my wife get help."

I'm not ashamed about being recognized in the community for what I did while high on prescribed meds. It's just that I've always been the reliable, behind-the-scene, figure in the crowd, the one to whom people come to help sort out their own problems, the one whom everyone trusts to be "normal." It's my loss of normalcy that bothers me most about my ten years with the diagnosis of Parkinson's and subsequent toxicity from the medications I needlessly took.

If I had a mere inkling that my symptoms were related to the medications rather than the disease itself, I would have requested a re-examination of my entire situation.

I remember telling Dr. Leo early in our relationship, "I don't care how shaky I get, I just don't want to lose my mind."

Greg asked, "In all those years, didn't you ever stop taking your pills?"

"No, I'm a nurse. I taught my patients to be compliant and I never missed a single day."

My response was filled with self-righteous indignation. Of course I took my meds every day – not on time necessarily but by the end of the day there were no pills remaining in the little compartments.

What a bloody stupid fool.

How many other patients, I wonder, are in the same situation I was in? How many physicians are prescribing anti Parkinson's medications without occasionally checking for rising homocysteine levels? How many families are watching loved ones become demented, thinking that the cause is the disease when a change in medications may make the difference? How much better would I be if someone had recognized sooner that my illness, my symptoms and my drugs just didn't jive? How many medical centers are ignoring the obvious to keep the numbers up in their research studies? What brain autopsy findings, I wonder, would the medical center have reported to my family, if I had actually died?

Yes, thanks to doctors I trusted, I've been given the opportunity to understand the problems of the mentally ill, from a whole different perspective. I now know why it is so hard for addicts to stay clean and why manic-depressives fight coming off the high side of their rollercoaster lives. I know what it's like to be the one without a key on a locked unit.

My hero, Dr. Fielding, left the medical center less than a year after he came to my rescue. He went back to the hospital where he completed his fellowship. Their gain, for sure.

* * *

In *The Third Wheel,* I wrote of Dan as a catalyst who came along at the right time. He gave me the opportunity to take risks again. Our summer of 2002 was the chain in the cycle that pulls this history along. I've always been a risk-taker, and I've always tried to help people. Helping him gave balance to my life and helped me feel richer and wiser. Though I was older in body than I should have been for my age, he made me feel younger in spirit.

Dan was right when he saw some of his behavior in me. Dopamine is one of those neurotransmitters that relates closely to the pleasure center of the brain. Truth be told, for a long time, I liked the increasing high I was experiencing. I loved the sense of energy, creativity and passion. *"Without passion,"* I wrote in a 2001 poem, *"life is flat, replete with routine, convenient for others, and signals the beginning of the end."* Gambling, hypersexuality, and other risky behaviors are now being reported fairly commonly with people taking Parkie meds.

When Dan left for rehab, he returned my laptop and I gave him a farewell poem. It was a summary of our summer, with a photo of our kayak island as backdrop. It ended where we started: *And remember, kindred souls live eternal in our hearts and minds... and when lonely, there are special places to go alone to be together... like the little island with all the driftwood... and then just listen to those angels, the ones without wings... you'll hear me, if you choose to listen... and I'll hear you.*

Dan has continued to stay at the program after finishing his own rehab. First, he became a counselor and then he was promoted to a management role. Some might say he has become addicted to Scientology as others find attending multiple AA/NA meetings per week provides them succor. Whatever, I'm just glad he's alive, clean, and working.

I sometimes wonder if his mind ever wanders back to Bethany. I hope he is still writing.

* * *

Our kids and their families came for Thanksgiving. It was such a warm, comfortable couple of days. "Do you remember before, when we'd come up?" Kim kidded Greg. "Just being around Mum for a few hours, that little vein in the top of your head would pop out as though it would burst."

"Oh God, Mum," Greg responded, looking at me to make sure it was alright to tease, "If I had to listen to your calling me every night to recite yet another poem, I think I'd have been the one on the psych unit!"

Then they gave us the news.

They had arranged for us all to go to Disney World in January. It was better than winning the Super Bowl!

* * *

When I first started to write poetry after having to retire from the job I loved, there was one that particularly reflected my attitude. It was inspired by the piece of glass sculpture my colleagues gave me at my roast.

Changed by the waves of farewell,
The hand-off complete

Constrained by years of corporate conformity,
Playing the game, living the role

Exhilarated by the sound of ocean waves,
Pounding the ground, knowing no bound

Suddenly freed to be flawed,
Picking the plays, making the rules

Struck by the wave of change,
The baton is seized.

It didn't take me long after "after Parkinson's" to seize my new life. And what a rich life I have now. Ike and I are closer than we have ever been. We see our kids often, because they enjoy being with us, not out of a sense of duty. And I brag about the four little granddaughters we now have, just like any other Granny.

And I will never forget their birthdays.

Normalcy is gradually returning. I don't go out nearly as often as I used to. But I have maintained most of my relationships with my artsy and musician friends. The guys in *lower case blues*, in particular, are doing just great. They've just released their third CD, *Days to Come* and it's terrific. On the night of the release party at the Rusty Rudder, they called me up on stage, introduced me as the fourth member of the band, and gave me an award "for your loving support." Soon they'll be national names, I just know it!

I'm still known around town for riding my three wheel bicycle. And I still love to kayak – the regular kind hurts my back so I got a neat new one that allows me to pedal with my feet and steer with a hand rudder rather than traditional paddling. I can't describe the joy I get from being alone on the water, laying back in my seat, scrunching my eyes as I gaze at the sky, and just listening to the sounds of nature.

Only Ike knows this, but together, we've got in the habit of laughing – at nothing! We watched a TV show about the power of laughter to release natural endorphins that keep you happy well after the laughter has stopped. We tried it and found it works! Usually we laugh aloud early in the morning to the amusement of Topper who tries to join in. Sometimes, when I'm walking on the beach, one arm still swinging and the other not, I turn around to check that no one is in the vicinity. Then, as the sanderlings dart back and forth with mechanical precision in the ebb and flow of the tide, their skinny, little legs racing faster than the eye can see, I start singing, loudly, totally out of tune.

> *I know a fat old policeman*
> *He's always on our street*
> *A fat and jolly red-faced man*
> *He really is a treat*
> *A ha ha ha ha ha ha ha ha*
> *Ooo hoo hoo hoo ha ha ha ha ha ha*

It's called a laughing song and was written at the height of the Music Hall era in London. It was sung in the depth of tube stations during the Blitz of World War II where it brought cheer at the worst time. I learned it at sing-songs at my parents' parties when I was growing up. It got people laughing then and it gets me laughing today!

And three times every week, you can still find me aqua-exercising at the pool with my same older lady friends. Marilyn doesn't get around as well any more although she still says she feels "swell" when asked! Sometimes we go to the library and the grocery store together, and we drink many cups of tea and a few tots of whiskey at her house. Occasionally we visit a friend of hers who is in a nursing home with Alzheimer's disease. When the door locks behind us and I look at the patients sitting with searching eyes watching soap operas they don't see, I imagine the person I thought would be me.

I confess that occasionally I do miss my dopamine high. Mostly, it is the mental energy that I'd like to have a bit more of. Sometimes, I have to talk myself into acknowledging that just because one is normal doesn't mean life has to be boring or lived without passion. It's just that it's time to move on. I have the rest of my life to do what I've always tried to do, my best.

* * *

As part of finishing this book, I stopped by "Ancient Art Tattoo." This time I told Ike in advance and teased him I'd come home with a matching tattoo on my other wrist. "Right," he said, knowing better.

"You look great," said Peggi. "And you're still wearing your hip glasses!"

"The lenses have been changed a couple of times," I responded, "but I still love the frames."

"So how are you, really?" she asked.

"I'm such a lucky woman, freed from drugs to be flawed in whatever I choose to do," I responded.

"I've brought you something," she said, handing me an envelope. Two photos were inside. One was a close up of my tattoo, the ink still glistening, and the other was of me sitting in her chair, my tattooed wrist in my lap. I was wearing a denim sleeveless shirt, short denim skirt and my same Moroccan red shoes. My face was expressionless and my eyes were vacant as I stared away from the camera. I forgot she took the pictures and I forgot what I was wearing. It was eerie to see how I looked just hours before I almost died.

She chuckled when I said, "That was the start of the craziness," and asked, "Did you bring me the poem?" When I removed the folded page from my pocket she added, "Read it aloud to me, please, for old times' sake."

I held the paper in my right hand. Below the tattoo, a bracelet dangles from my wrist. Kim gave it to me the day after I was transferred back to the medical center, before the truth was known. The bracelet is adorned with colored stones, each with a saying. The one that is used as a clasp is the reason Kim bought it for me. It reads, *"Live Your Poem."* Oh Kim, I try, every day.

> *They glance, beware*
> *and look away*
> *before they stare*
> *and gingerly stroke*
> *my wrist*
> *with finger tip*
> *outstretched,*
> *as though it might*
> *rub off,*
> *on them.*

*"It's real," they exclaim,
"how neat, so cool,
I want one too!" or,
"Did it hurt? How brave,
to break the rule!" or
"It's vile to defile
what God has given you."
But whatever their opinion,
each asks, as was my intention,
"What does it mean?"*

*"Think clone...think cure,"
I read and explain.
"It's a statement.
"Stem cells cloned
make healthy cells
to cure Parkinson's, paralysis,
multiple sclerosis,
but the research is
banned, unfunded,
wrongly discredited."*

*"How can that be?"
most ask,
as ignorant
in their bliss as the
one, morally remiss,
who uses the unborn
to blaspheme the living
disabled,
preventing scientific proof
becoming therapeutic truth.*

*A tattoo,
etched out of the blue,*

a permanent needling
of judgment askew,
mine and theirs.
They, who mis-prescribed,
doping me out of my mind;
me ever intent
on making a difference
in a world, indifferent.

The Tattoo is the last poem I wrote. My spark of creativity was apparently fueled by the excess of dopamine. But now, hallelujah, I can concentrate to read again! I can cuddle my lovely little granddaughters and focus my mind purely on them. I can now even enjoy the simple things in life, like watching television with Ike.

As the old English expression goes, "What you lose on the roundabout, you gain on the swings..."

* * *

Ike and I still sleep in our same bed and, despite the admonitions of police officers to Ike to remove all sharp objects from our house, his hunting knife remains in the headboard.

He bought new sheets by the time I got home from the hospital but by the time the cold nights of late fall appeared, he found me looking through the linen closet for our electric under-blanket. He gave it to me a few Christmas' ago and I loved it.

"You're wasting your time," he said. "It was on the bed that night, saturated, so I threw it away."

It took about a year to purchase a new mattress. The four separate blood stains haunted me very time I changed the sheets. The biggest one had been under my left groin. It soaked all the way through to the under side. The ones from my neck had been partially absorbed by my pillow but joined together with a narrow strip like a weird Rorschach design.

Eventually, we decided that my restless, achy legs warranted the purchase of a new, larger mattress. We were back to shared purchasing decisions, and spur of the moment eBay bids were a thing of the past. We bought a queen size mattress this time. He and Topper like it better because I don't kick them so much. But it's not as conducive to snuggling!

Ike surreptitiously checks me every night after I go to bed and he stays up to watch TV. He didn't know I was aware of it until, as I finished writing this book, I brought it to his attention. "That night is forever etched in my little brain," he said.

Trust disrupted is as antithetical to one's sense of normalcy as the scarred face in the mirror of a person with third degree burns.

Thanks for taking care of me, Ike. Life may not be that rose garden, but fallen petals make for soft landings. And we sure have planted and nourished some great seeds in our own back yard.

Epilogue

Last, but not least, if my writing has touched you in any way, please jump on the bandwagon:

1. To promote stem cell research. So many conditions have the potential to be radically improved through this means. I believe it.

   The Stem Cell Action Network is the best organization I know to provide information and promote action. Their website is www. stemcellaction.org

2. To prevent suicide. I was lucky to survive my attempt. It is the 10th highest cause of death in Delaware. More than the loss of the individual, suicide devastates families.

   The National Suicide Prevention Lifeline' hotline is open 24/7 at 1-800-273-TALK (8255).

3. To find a cure for Parkinson's disease. Once again, I am lucky to have escaped this debilitating disease, at least for now.

   The Michael J. Fox Foundation for Parkinson's Research is a great source of information at www.michaeljfox.org

Thank you.

About the author

Christina Weaver authored numerous articles published in professional journals during her career as a nurse executive and healthcare technology and management consultant. In retirement, she has published over fifty articles on entertainment and healthcare in local newspapers and magazines. She self published a book of her poetry and photographs, *Delaware I Sing of Thy Shore*, and has another completed manuscript on the subject of Belief. *What You Lose on the Roundabout,* a memoir, is her first full-length book. Christina and her husband, Ike, celebrate their 40th wedding anniversary this year, 2007, surrounded by their close family and numerous friends.

www.cgweaver.com

CPSIA information can be obtained at www.ICGtesting.com
Printed in the USA
BVOW06s0239230616

453176BV00011B/85/P